Where'd THAT come from?!

Everyday Expressions Found in THE BIBLE

Steven Melvin McCalip

Where'd That Come From?

ISBN 0-89957-359-2

Cover Design: The Williams Company
Editing: Dr. Warren Baker, Dan Penwell, and Richard A. Steele
Page Layout: Richard A. Steele

Printed in Canada
07 06 05 04 03 02 –T– 7 6 5 4 3 2

To all those who believe:

"The law of the LORD is perfect, converting the soul: the testimony of LORD is sure, making wise the simple. . . . More to be desired are they than gold, yea, than much fine gold: Sweeter also than honey, and the honeycomb." (Psalm 19:7, 10)

Contents

Preface

It's been stated that more books have been written about the Bible than about any other topic. Of all those books, I have seen only a handful that touched on the topic of common sayings occurring in the Bible. However, none of those books covered the topic to the extent and in the manner I thought the Bible deserved. Some of those books bog readers down with archaic words and literary allusions from the Bible (i.e., "husbandman," "sottish," "burning bush," "lilies of the field," etc.) and some emphasized popular quotations like "O ye of little faith" and "Why hast thou forsaken me?"

I wanted my book to focus solely on **common sayings,** so I set out to find as many of these expressions that occurred in the Bible as I could. I also wanted to distinguish popular expressions in current usage from those that were more popular in previous generations. It has been an exhausting yet thoroughly enjoyable task. Reading through just about every occurrence of every word in *Strong's Exhaustive Concordance of the Bible* can be tedious to say the least. Reading through the entire Bible again in my search for these phrases, however, has been very rewarding. Even after several years and hundreds of sayings later, I am to this day still finding more familiar sayings in the Bible. I'm sure the reader will share the joy of finding new ones as well.

I think *Where'd That Come From?* is another example of why the Bible itself is such a unique and influential book. It is my love for the King James Version of the Bible that gave me the desire to have this work published. I can't tell you how many times these expressions have opened a door to discuss the deeper issues of the Bible with others.

First and foremost, my deepest gratitude goes out to the best-selling author of all time, the Lord Jesus Christ, for giving me the love for His book and the passion to write about the "wondrous things out of thy law" (Ps. 119:18). I also want to express my gratitude to my wife Lisa and our children—Andrew, Jonathan, Samuel, and Jacob—for their patience, understanding, and encouragement and for helping me stick to this project and see its fruition. Their belief in the need for this book made all the difference. Special thanks go out to my other family members and friends who supported my efforts. *Where'd That Come From?* truly is a "labor of love" given to me by the Lord for His book.

Introduction

Throughout recorded history, perhaps no language has exercised more worldwide influence than the English language. Over the last five hundred years, English has become the universal tongue and official language in world politics, public education, scientific research, and international commerce. Even more importantly, it has become the primary or secondary language in just about every corner of the globe.

When one considers the impact of the English language, a question worth pondering is this: What propelled and contributed to English becoming such a dominant language in the world? The rise of England to world power status through its global colonization is one logical explanation that comes to mind. What is not given its just due, however, is the influence of England's Bible, the King James Version, on our written and spoken English.

Translated in 1611, the King James Bible soon became the standard by which all other translations measure themselves. It has been, and continues to be, the single greatest selling and most widely distributed book of all time. It is, as some have aptly said, "the book that shook the world." Its contributions to Western literature are practically immeasurable, being mentioned by many of the world's most renowned writers as having a profound effect on them and their writings. The individual books of Job and Psalms, among others, have been called the finest examples of poetry ever penned, and this is said by many who don't claim to be Christians.

Although there is a great need to show all of the various contributions of the King James Bible to the English language, one aspect that deserves particular attention is the influence of this Bible on our common speech. Whether we be Christian, Muslim, Buddhist, agnostic, or atheist, we all incorporate a host of biblical sayings into our daily conversations.

The English language is replete with idioms, sayings, and expressions of which a surprising number originate or were made popular from the King James Version of the Bible. The words of this Bible translation have become imbedded in our common speech, yet we often speak biblical phrases daily without realizing we are quoting from or alluding directly to the King James Bible. Sayings such as "rise and shine," "give up the ghost," "the skin of your teeth," "see eye to eye," "safe and sound," and "eat, drink, and be merry" are just several of the hundreds of examples in this work.

The King James Bible is the most widely recognized, the most widely memorized, and the most widely read book in the world. The book speaks for itself quite literally. It is "high time" (Romans 13:11) that we recognize its hold on our language.

Jesus said, "The words that I speak unto you, they are spirit, and they are life." Despite being thousands of years old, His words are most assuredly living in today's language. Well-known expressions such as "the blind leading the blind," "the powers that be," and "fall by the wayside," are, as the book of Isaiah says, "a drop in the bucket" compared to the five hundred or more popular sayings that are in our Bible.

It is my belief that a majority of these expressions did come or were made popular from Scripture. I base this opinion mainly on the Bible's age and its pervasive influence on many languages, especially English. The manuscripts that produced the King James Version of the Bible go back as far as thirty-five hundred years! Most of recorded history begins not long before that, so the Bible has been influencing the language of mankind for longer than just about any other written source.

In preparing this book, I chose the sayings that I felt were most often used based on my personal experience and research. The sayings used are all considered to be popular at one time or another by various authorities of English language studies. Of course, all Scripture quotations found in this book are from the King James Version.

A major portion of this work has been dedicated to showing the biblical context of these phrases. Each phrase is highlighted in the Scripture in which it occurs, and each phrase's meaning (when not obvious) is discussed as well. The subject matter of the surrounding verses and their occasionally controversial doctrines are often discussed. It is not my intention to promote strife or antagonize, yet it is my desire to give my understanding of the context of these phrases and how they relate to the issues of the day.

Readers will appreciate the various appendices found in this work that show additional expressions and their cultural usage. Appendix A lists expressions that were more popular in past years, and Appendix B includes phrases that are alluded to in the Bible; that is, those that are hinted at but not directly stated. Appendices C and D show how these expressions have been used in motion picture and song titles in Western culture. Not included is a list of book titles having biblical expressions, for that could have filled another whole book. Suffice it to say that thousands of these expressions have been used as the titles of books over the years.

It is my hope that after you have read this work, you will gain a newfound appreciation and respect for the Bible and its immense, profound, and unending spiritual and cultural impact on American society and the world.

Steven M. McCalip

A

act of God

But your eyes have seen all the great **acts of the Lord** *which he did.* (Deuteronomy 11:7)

Moses reminded Israel of all the "great acts of the Lord" which they had seen including the drowning of Pharaoh and his army in the Red Sea. Also called a great act of the Lord was the literal opening up of the earth and the swallowing of the households of Dathan and Abiram for their rebellion against God. This incident foreshadowed the fate of the wicked who will actually be cast into the same place as Dathan and Abiram's household—the middle of the earth, or hell, according to many scriptures. Psalm 55:15 says the wicked "go down quick into hell," and Jesus said in Luke 10:15 that people are "thrust down to hell." "The way of life *is* above to the wise, that he may depart from hell beneath" (Proverbs 15:24).

Insurance companies today refuse to cover acts of God, or natural calamities, as they label it. Apparently, they aren't responsible for what God does. The Lord offers fire and life insurance of a different sort, but unlike others, He covers "acts of God."

all things are possible

And Jesus looking upon them saith, With men it is impossible, but not with God: for with God **all things are possible**. (Mark 10:27)

People like to think that all things are possible concerning man's abilities, but according to the Bible, the phrase "all things are possible" is true only with God. Jesus made this statement in response to a question from His disciples as to whom could be saved. The Lord had just told them that it was very difficult for a rich man to enter heaven, but with God this was not impossible. If nothing were impossible for man, we wouldn't need God. We should be thankful for the things that are impossible for us, for these things force us to go to God.

all things to all men

To the weak became I as weak, that I might gain the weak: I am made **all things to all men**, *that I might by all means save some.* (1 Corinthians 9:22)

This expression is mistakenly understood by some Christians to mean that beliefs can be compromised in order to get along with others for the ultimate purpose of getting people saved. A Christian shouldn't lie in order to befriend a liar; he shouldn't become worldly in order to win the world. Paul spoke of winning souls, not by any means necessary, but by becoming a servant to others.

The seasoned saint learns to become all things to all people by taking on the different roles of a Christian such as a teacher who explains the scriptures, a fisherman who fishes for souls, a farmer who tends his crops, and a soldier who practices warfare.

There are many other roles that allow the Christian to truly become "all things to all men." The Christian's life, therefore, is a mastery of numerous occupations, making the believer a jack-of-all-trades and a master of *many*. If you truly want a well-rounded education, try Christianity.

all to the good

And we know that **all things work together for good** *to them that love God, to them who are the called according to his purpose.* (Romans 8:28)

Everybody's heard the advice that "everything will work out for the better." Once again, this expression is true only if that person is a believer according to the verse of scripture above—"to them that love God." Unbelievers who claim this promise are deceiving themselves and others. This expression is usually spoken when something awful has happened and someone is trying to comfort himself or others.

The next time you hear this phrase used, you might want to tell that person that things aren't going to work out for him if he's not a Christian. Of course, you'll then be bombarded with how judgmental you are. That's when the believer needs to remind this person that Paul prayed that our love "may abound yet more and more in knowledge and *in* all judgment" (Philippians 1:9). Things may work out for an unbeliever, but they won't work out for his or her good.

apple of one's eye

He found him in a desert land, and in the waste howling wilderness; he led him about, he instructed him, he kept him as **the apple of his eye**. (Deuteronomy 32:10)

Moses described God's feelings about Israel in the book of Deuteronomy as "the apple of His eye." Anything or anyone that is considered dear to another is termed the "apple of one's eye." God considered Israel dear to Him, not because Israel was better than the other nations, but, as God said, to fulfill His plan for the redemption of mankind. This plan was promised to Abraham and his descendants, which is Israel.

Jews refer to themselves as "the chosen people," but they must remember that God could have chosen any nation to carry out His plan. Another reason God chose Israel was to confound the wise with the fact that a tiny nation such as Israel could play such a major part in the history and future of the world. Just witness the entire Mideast crisis, and you will see that the entire conflict all revolves around who will control the city of Jerusalem—the Muslims, the Jews, or the Christians. It is no accident that Jerusalem has been center stage in world history, and according to Revelation, it will be once again. Stay tuned.

as a tree falls, so shall it lay

If the clouds be full of rain, they empty themselves upon the earth: and if the tree fall toward the south, or toward the north, in the place **where the tree falleth, there it shall be.** (Ecclesiastes 11:3)

An expected happening or a natural result of a situation can be described by saying, "As a tree falls, so shall it lay." Another similar saying would be, "The apple doesn't fall very far from the tree."

When a tree falls, its end is final. It's not going to prop itself back up.

The same analogy applies in our lives. The Bible often compares trees to people. We can devise many things to manipulate the direction of our lives, and to say to ourselves, "there is still time," but once we die, the chance for repentance is gone (Revelation 22:11).

as good as dead

Therefore sprang there even of one, and him **as good as dead,** *so many as the stars of the sky in multitude, and as the sand which is by the sea shore innumerable.* (Hebrews 11:12)

God promised Abraham, the patriarch of Israel that from his seed would come the Messiah, the savior of the world. Abraham had reached one hundred years of age, but he and Sarah were still childless. God then decided to give Sarah a child, and she "received strength to conceive seed" (Hebrews 11:11). One hundred-year-old people having babies today would be quite a spectacle.

This story foreshadowed the birth of Jesus Christ, who, of course, was born miraculously of the virgin Mary. To be "as good as dead" is to be under the same conditions as death or similar to them. The birth of Abraham and Sarah's child Isaac also showed how God likes to bring life out of death, thereby teaching us the principle of life after death.

Spiritually speaking, people who don't know Jesus should also be considered "as good as dead" because the Bible says they are "dead" in their trespasses and sins. Though horror movies make fun of the idea of dead people walking, the dead do indeed walk the earth today, and this should also cause us to be horrified.

(ashes to ashes), dust to dust

*In the sweat of thy face shalt thou eat bread, till thou return unto the ground; for out of it wast thou taken: for **dust** thou art, and un**to dust** shalt thou return.* (Genesis 3:19)

As a result of Adam's disobedience in the garden, God cursed man with physical death and strenuous labor, neither of which existed at that time according to Genesis. Since God created man out of dust, death would result in man going back to dust. Yes, we are made of the dust, but combined with God's breath of life, we are living beings.

at death's door

*Have the gates of death been opened unto thee? or hast thou seen the **doors** of the shadow **of death**?* (Job 38:17)

We use the saying "at death's door" to speak of someone about to die. In the midst of Job's suffering and complaints, God answered him with a series of questions, one of which was "Hast thou seen the doors of the shadow of death?" Just like there are literal gates of pearl, or pearly gates, there are also the gates of hell, which are the doors of death. To say someone is "at death's door" is to speak of one's imminent death.

These doors have locks and keys according to Revelation 1:18 where Jesus says, I "have the keys of hell and death." Life boils down to choosing the right door.

Jesus also said, "I am the door" implying that there are many doors to choose from, but He is "the" only one that leads to eternal life.

at your wits' end

They reel to and fro, and stagger like a drunken man, and are **at their wits' end**. *Then they cry unto the* LORD *in their trouble, and he bringeth them out of their distresses.* (Psalm 107:27–28)

A stark picture of God's view of the heathen is shown here in the book of Psalms. In this passage of Scripture the psalmist compares the lost to "a drunken man" and to a ship in a stormy sea (vv. 23–25). The psalmist also said they would call on the Lord when they reach "their wits' end." What an indictment of human nature that comment is! Man will only seek God when he has reached his wit's end, or the point of absolute desperation.

It is only when man has exhausted his own "wits" that he comes to God. That is a good thing, for our "wits" can't save us. Our knowledge is not sufficient to reach Him. We must all reach our wit's end and rely on God's wits if we truly seek to be saved. Needless to say, God's wits do not have an end.

B

baptism of fire

I indeed baptize you with water unto repentance: but he that cometh after me is mightier than I, whose shoes I am not worthy to bear: he shall __baptize__ you with the Holy Ghost, and __with fire__: (Matthew 3:11)

Some religious people talk of being "baptized with the Holy Ghost and fire," not realizing that to be "baptized with fire" means to go to hell. The next verse proves this assertion by stating that "he will burn up the chaff with unquenchable fire." The chaff is described in other references as the lost, and the unquenchable fire is the same fire Jesus mentions in Mark chapter 9, where He speaks of someone losing his soul and going to hell where the "fire is not quenched."

Secular people use this phrase to refer to someone being thrown into the middle of a task for the first time and experiencing all the suffering that goes with it. This secular interpretation actually comes closer to the real definition of the phrase than the modern religious interpretation.

be about your business

And he said unto them, How is it that ye sought me? wist ye not that I must __be about my__ Father's __business__? (Luke 2:49)

Mary and Joseph were looking for Jesus and found Him in the temple. The twelve-year-old so amazed the scholars and priests in the temple that the Bible said they were "astonished at his understanding and answers" (Luke 2:47). Jesus explained to His parents that He was just going about His Father's business.

People will tell you to go about your business if you're bothering them or if they feel you are meddling in their affairs. Sometimes, we Christians forget that we should make the Father's business, which is to preach the gospel, our business.

be of good cheer

These things have I spoken unto you, that in me ye might have peace. In the world ye shall have tribulation: but **be of good cheer;** *I have overcome the world.* (John 16:33)

Jesus Christ is the only man to have ever overcome every temptation put against Him, and when His Spirit dwells in us, and we yield to it, we can be of good cheer because we now have the power to overcome these temptations also. The "Don't worry, be happy" crowd should be very worried and very unhappy. They are rejecting the only person that can give them happiness.

beat the air

I therefore so run, not as uncertainly; so fight I, not as one that **beateth the air.** (1 Corinthians 9:26)

Other expressions similar to "beating the air" include "spinning your wheels" and "banging your head against a wall." The unbeliever is referred to as "beating the air" because he doesn't know his true purpose in life or how to obtain it. He is in the proverbial "rat race" and is running in circles. Conversely, the Christian knows the meaning and purpose of life through this one verse: "I am the way, the truth, and the life." Those nine words can stop you in a hurry from "spinning your wheels," "banging your head against a wall," and "beating the air."

become a byword

And thou shalt **become** *an astonishment, a proverb, and* **a byword**, *among all nations whither the* LORD *shall lead thee.* (Deuteronomy 28:37)

God served warning on Israel that if they refused to walk according to His laws, He would curse everything to do with them. "Cursed *shalt* thou *be* when thou comest in, and cursed *shalt* thou *be* when thou goest out" (Deut. 28:19). God gave the law to Israel, not to see if they could keep it, but to show them that they couldn't because of their inherent sinfulness.

What Israel failed to recognize, and what man today also fails to recognize, is that only one Person could keep the law without ever breaking it. Perfection is the only standard God will accept, and anybody who thinks he is pleasing God with good deeds apart from faith will receive the same curses as those of Israel.

God doesn't weigh your good deeds against your bad, and even if He did, everyone would fail that test as well. To "become a byword" means the same as it did in biblical days—to be notorious or infamous, just like Israel after God got through dealing with them.

bent out of shape

For we would not, brethren, have you ignorant of our trouble which came to us in Asia, that we were **pressed** **out of measure**, *above strength, insomuch that we despaired even of life.* (2 Corinthians 1:8)

"Pressed out of measure's" modern equivalent, "bent out of shape," has changed slightly from its biblical meaning of being pushed to the limit, referring now to someone who gets upset over a matter rather easily. The apostle Paul was so pressed out of measure that he said he "despaired even of life." Yes, even the great Paul had times, when, despite his faith and calling to God's work, he was sure his death was an inevitable consequence of his circumstances. What is our reaction when we feel we are "bent out of shape"?

beside yourself

And when his friends heard of it, they went out to lay hold on him: for they said, He is **beside himself.** (Mark 3:21)

Jesus was falsely accused of many things in His day, one of which was being crazy. This accusation came from His so-called "friends" who wanted to apprehend Him. In Mark 3, Jesus spent time healing the sick and casting out unclean spirits, actions that upset the establishment of that day and caused the Pharisees to believe that He was beside Himself, or just plain crazy.

bid someone Godspeed

Whosoever transgresseth and abideth not in the doctrine of Christ, hath not God. He that abideth in the doctrine of Christ, he hath both the Father and the Son. If there come any unto you, and bring not this doctrine, receive him not into your house, neither **bid him God speed***: For he that biddeth him God speed is partaker of his evil deeds.* (2 John 9–11)

A careful reading of these verses would shock most people, for they fly in the face of what is taught even by the Christian establishment, and certainly the secular world. First off, having Jesus Christ *is* having the Father and the Son. Secondly, you are commanded not to let people into your home who teach false doctrine. It doesn't even matter if you're trying to win them to Christ. Thirdly, we are commanded not to wish these people Godspeed, which is to wish them God's blessings, in other words, to wish them well. To do so, John says, makes us an accessory to their "evil deeds."

bitter end

*For the lips of a strange woman drop as an honeycomb, and her mouth is smoother than oil: But her **end is bitter** as wormwood, sharp as a twoedged sword.* (Proverbs 5:3–4)

The Bible describes the consequences of casual sex in this warning about promiscuous women. Solomon warns us of the whorish woman, saying that she talks sweet as honey, but "her end is bitter as wormwood." She is also described as a "twoedged sword," another biblical expression referred to later in this work.

Those mentioned in Scripture who engaged in casual sex are not deemed as "fooling around" or having "affairs," but are labeled as "whores" (see Ezekiel 16:33; Proverbs 6:26; Revelation 21:8 etc.). The Bible tells it like it is and doesn't mince words about immoral sexual conduct.

blind leading the blind

*Let them alone: they be blind leaders of the blind. And if the **blind lead the blind**, both shall fall into the ditch.* (Matthew 15:14)

One of the most popular of all biblical clichés is this one that Jesus used to characterize the Pharisees, the religious leaders of His day. After being informed that the Pharisees were offended at Him, Jesus told His disciples that these hypocrites were "blind leaders of the blind," and that they would end up in the ditch. When Jesus called them "blind," He was teaching that they were spiritually blind, that is, lost sinners, and not only they, but also their followers. You can't cure blindness by pretending to see, and the same applies spiritually.

The situation is no different today, just the names of the organizations have changed. If you want to pattern your life after Jesus, you should expect to have the same confrontations and the same enemies as He. We would never seek directions from a physically blind person, so why do so many seek guidance from the spiritually blind? The answer may be that if you're physically blind, there's no way you can absolutely know if someone else is also. The same holds true in the spiritual realm, and that's why we need Jesus, who makes the blind to see.

blood on your hands

And when ye spread forth your hands, I will hide mine eyes from you: yea, when ye make many prayers, I will not hear: <u>your hands are full of blood</u>. (Isaiah 1:15)

God told Israel that He was sick of their burnt offerings and sacrifices: "To what purpose *is* the multitude of your sacrifices unto me? saith the LORD: I am full of the burnt offerings of rams, and the fat of fed beasts; and I delight not in the blood of bullocks, or of lambs, or of he goats . . . your new moons and your appointed feasts my soul hateth" (Isaiah 1:11, 14).

Paul confirmed God's hatred for animal sacrifices in the New Testament when he said in Hebrews 10:6: "In burnt offerings and *sacrifices* for sin thou hast had no pleasure." Though God instructed Israel to offer sacrifices, it might be asked, "Why then does He say He is sick of them?" God was sick of them because Israel was relying on the sacrifice to make them holy instead of focusing upon what the sacrifice pointed to: the ultimate sacrifice of Jesus on the cross. In Hebrews 10:12, it states: "But this man, after he had offered one sacrifice for sins for ever, sat down on the right hand of God."

The phrase "blood on your hands" signifies that a person is guilty of a matter and that there is evidence (blood) to prove it.

blow your own horn

Therefore when thou doest thine alms, do not <u>*sound a trumpet before*</u> <u>*thee*</u>*, as the hypocrites do in the synagogues and in the streets, that they* *may have glory of men. Verily I say unto you, They have their reward.* (Matthew 6:2)

Jesus said hypocrites like to "sound a trumpet" or "blow their own horns," and thereby brag about themselves or their accomplishments to others. The reason they do it, He says, is to get "glory of men," in other words, to get man's approval and praise.

One of the defining characteristics of a Christian is his refusal to be a "man pleaser." To a Christian, pleasing God is what matters. In Galatians 1:10, Paul said, "For do I now persuade men, or God? or do I seek to please men? for if I yet pleased men, I should not be the servant of Christ." Jesus said men who are this way "have their reward." What he implied is that their reward from God is null and void.

bottomless pit

And the fifth angel sounded, and I saw a star fall from heaven unto the earth: and to him was given the key of the **bottomless pit**. (Revelation 9:1)

According to Revelation, the "bottomless pit" is the place inside of the earth filled with smoke and locusts—possibly an allusion to hell or the lake of fire. The implication of the phrase is a warning to unbelievers that hell cannot be too full for them—their punishment will not be commuted due to overcrowding.

The world, has taken this phrase and obscured its original implication to now refer to a person who can eat and eat and never get full.

breach of promise

And the number of the days in which ye searched the land, even forty days, each day for a year, shall ye bear your iniquities, even forty years, and ye shall know my **breach of promise**. (Numbers 14:34)

As used today, this adage denotes someone who breaks his word with another party. As God used it, He spoke of His promise made to Israel about them inheriting the land. Fulfillment of this promise would be delayed because of Israel's constant complaining of there being "giants in the land."

You'd probably be a little apprehensive also if you had just seen nine and ten-foot people who didn't want you around. Yes, there were giants in the Bible, and there is ample evidence outside the scriptures that they existed.

The Bible also mentions "monsters" and "dragons," and if you think these are just exaggerations or figurative speech, you ought to read your Bible more carefully. They're not. It is correct, then, to say that Christians believe in giants, monsters, ghosts, devils, talking snakes, and many other so-called fairy tales (see **give up the ghost**). God tests our faith and fear of man with these types of beliefs.

break bread

And upon the first day of the week, when the disciples came together to **break bread**, *Paul preached unto them, ready to depart on the morrow; and continued his speech until midnight.* (Acts 20:7)

Sharing a meal together is the equivalent of "breaking bread," and this phrase is usually used between close friends as it was with Paul and his disciples. Jesus spoke of Himself as the "bread of life," and in the same discourse in John chapter six, He said, "Whoso eateth my flesh, and drinketh my blood, hath eternal life; and I will raise him up at the last day" (John 6:54).

Eternal life, ironically, *is* connected with eating. What does it mean, then, to eat His flesh, since this teaching is connected to eternal life? John 6:63 provides the answer, and it connects the disciples' misunderstanding of Jesus' command to eat His flesh to Jesus' own interpretation of what He meant. Jesus said, "It is the spirit that quickeneth; the <u>flesh</u> profiteth nothing: the words that I speak unto you, they are spirit and they are life." The flesh Christ talks about eating are His *words*, of which we symbolically eat when we believe them as it is stated in Jeremiah 15:16: "Thy words were found, and I did eat them."

break of day

When he therefore was come up again, and had broken bread, and eaten, and talked a long while, even till **break of day***, so he departed.* (Acts 20:11)

Also referred to as "daybreak," "crack of dawn," and so forth, this idiom was used similarly in the book of Acts. Paul almost literally talked a man to death who was listening to him preach. This man was up on the loft where Paul was preaching and got so tired he fell and nearly died. Paul had been preaching all night and into the morning hours (the "break of day").

People sure seem to get sleepy during sermons, but when's the last time you heard all-night preaching? It was nothing unusual in the early church. America likes its sermons about twenty minutes long with lots of jokes and stories and a scripture verse every now and then that's not offensive. Microwave Christianity—just add water and mix.

break your heart

Then Paul answered, What mean ye to weep and to **break mine heart***? for I am ready not to be bound only, but also to die at Jerusalem for the name of the Lord Jesus.* (Acts 21:13)

Paul's heart was broken after hearing that his disciples cried. They cried because they didn't want him to go to Jerusalem, for they feared the Jews would apprehend and put Paul in jail as they had before.

A broken heart is precisely what God uses to create a new heart. God has been giving heart transplants longer than any other doctor, and He will give anybody one that recognizes that his first heart is evil. As Jeremiah states, "The heart *is* deceitful above all *things*, and desperately wicked: who can know it?" (Jeremiah 17:10).

breathe new life into something

And the LORD *God formed man of the dust of the ground, and* **breathed into** *his nostrils the breath of* **life***; and man became a living soul.* (Genesis 2:7)

An accurate description of how God created man is depicted here as God actually did breathe life into Adam.

Today, when we speak of "breathing new life" into something, we mean that we're taking something that is old or worn out and reviving it. The use of this phrase "breathe new life" in its literal sense is an action that only God can do. It is only when this expression is used in a figurative sense that this ability can be attributed to man.

bring me word

And he sent them to Bethlehem, and said, Go and search diligently for the young child; and when ye have found him, **bring me word** *again, that I may come and worship him also.* (Matthew 2:8)

To bring word to someone is to deliver a message. Under the pretense of worshipping the Child, King Herod wanted to find Jesus, but his real desire was to kill Him. The wise men from the East agreed to tell Herod when they found Jesus, not knowing his plans. The wise men weren't as wise as they were cracked up to be. (Incidentally, the Scriptures don't say that there were *three* wise men, only that there were three kinds of gifts.)

bring someone's head on a platter

And **brought his head in a charger,** *and gave it to the damsel: and the damsel gave it to her mother.* (Mark 6:28)

If someone threatens to "bring your head on a platter," you know you messed up pretty badly. This story in the Bible refers to King Herod's birthday party when the king told his daughter he would give her almost anything she desired. After the daughter consulted with her mother, both agreed that they wanted the head of John the Baptist on a platter. Herod had already promised his daughter he would give her just about any request, so he honored it and had John beheaded.

What a testament to the influence of John the Baptist that the king's daughter could have had half her father's kingdom and she instead chose the death of this great man. What an indictment of the wicked also when their conscience wouldn't allow them to let a man of God live.

bring to light

Therefore judge nothing before the time, until the Lord come, who both will **bring to light** *the hidden things of darkness, and will make manifest the counsels of the hearts: and then shall every man have praise of God.* (1 Corinthians 4:5)

Any matter that will be brought to light means that all aspects of it will be brought under close scrutiny and revealed. Not only will the unbeliever be judged for his evil deeds, every one of his iniquities will be revealed to everyone else at the Great White Throne Judgment, including his thoughts. What a humiliating and frightening time that will be for the sinner!

Jesus also verified this coming day and said, "Fear them not therefore: for there is nothing covered, that shall not be revealed; and hid, that shall not be known" (Matthew 10:26). There are some who are exempt from this Judgment. Those who want an exemption will have to reconcile themselves with God first.

brother's keeper

And the LORD said unto Cain, Where is Abel thy brother? And he said, I know not: Am I **my brother's keeper***? (Genesis 4:9)*

The inevitable question asked by all big brothers, "Am I my brother's keeper?" was asked by Cain out of jealousy of his brother Abel. Cain and Abel both offered sacrifices to God, but God approved only of Abel's because Abel's was a blood sacrifice and Cain's wasn't. Cain knew that his own offering was wrong, so he tried to substitute his own brand of religion which God rejected.

This whole story exemplifies the futile attempts of any man who tries to come to God without accepting the ultimate blood sacrifice of God's own death on the cross. Anything else is a false, man-made religion that puts you in the same league as Cain, and we are to be "not as Cain," whom the Bible says "was of that wicked one, and slew his brother. And wherefore slew he him? Because his own works were evil, and his brother's righteous."

build on sand

And every one that heareth these sayings of mine, and doeth them not, shall be likened unto a foolish man, which **built** *his house* **upon the sand***: And the rain descended, and the floods came and the winds blew, and beat upon that house; and it fell: and great was the fall of it.* (Matthew 7:26–27)

Does this story sound familiar? Everyone remembers "The Three Little Pigs" that the wolf was chasing and how the wolf huffed and puffed and blew down two of the pigs' houses that were made of straw and wood. The wolf couldn't blow down the pig's house made of brick, just as the wind couldn't blow down the house built on the rock in Jesus' story.

The Bible shows up in the most unexpected of places, and we use its phrase "built on sand" to denote something that won't last. Nobody with any sense builds a house on sand, so why do we build our spiritual houses on them?

burnt offering

And Noah builded an altar unto the LORD; and took of every clean beast, and of every clean fowl, and offered **burnt offerings** *on the altar.* (Genesis 8:20)

The first thing Noah did when he got off the ark was build an altar. Keep in mind that Noah just got through living in the ark for almost an entire year before he was able to leave the boat. It is a testament to Noah's faith that after going through the most trying ordeal of his time he chose to give God thanks and build an altar unto Him.

The expression "burnt offering" is used jokingly to mean someone burnt the food being served. Though we've all had that experience of being served burnt food, let us remember that the first burnt offerings were for giving thanks.

by and by

Yet hath he not root in himself, but dureth for a while: for when tribulation or persecution ariseth because of the word, **by and by** *he is offended.* (Matthew 13:21)

In Jesus' parable of the sower, the sower plants four kinds of seeds, three of which bear no fruit and one that does. One of the seeds, interpreted as a person's heart, doesn't endure and is offended at the words of the Bible as it is stated in Matthew above.

One of the signs, then, of a wicked heart is a person that is offended at what Jesus calls "the Word," or the Scriptures. This offense can take on many forms, one of which includes casting doubt on the authenticity of the Bible.

by the letter

And shall not uncircumcision which is by nature, if it fulfil the law, judge thee, who **by the letter** *and circumcision dost transgress the law?* (Romans 2:27)

When you're a stickler for the rules, you're also said to "go by the book," or "by the letter" as it reads in Romans. Paul was chastising Jews who wanted to keep the practice of circumcision as a part of the requirements for salvation. He told them that salvation was a matter of circumcising your heart, not your body.

Spiritually speaking, circumcision was given by God as a token of the covenant between God and Abraham, but physically applied, circumcision keeps out infections that the uncircumcised may get from time to time.

by the skin of your teeth

My bone cleaveth to my skin and to my flesh, and I am escaped **with the skin of my teeth**. (Job 19:20)

Popping up constantly in modern conversation, "by the skin of your teeth" refers to anyone who just barely makes it by or escapes from some situation. This phrase is another example of how unaware people are that they quote the Scriptures in their everyday speech.

The story of Job tells of him barely escaping the calamities that befell his children. Job, of course, is famous for his patience, and his story is naturally where we get the phrase "the patience of Job" (see "patience of Job").

The book of Job is likely the oldest book in the Bible and one of the oldest in the world. Still, the King James English translation of this book continues to enrich us with numerous, colorful expressions such as "make the hair of your neck stand on end," "watch the sparks fly," "drink it like water," and many more.

by the sweat of your brow

In <u>the sweat of thy face</u> *shalt thou eat bread, till thou return unto the ground; for out of it wast thou taken: for dust thou art, and unto dust shalt thou return.* (Genesis 3:19)

Part of the original curse God placed on Adam was not work, as commonly thought, but strenuous work. Eve's curse also has been misconstrued as being childbearing, but a careful reading of Genesis shows her curse to be pain or "sorrow" in childbearing.

Today, women speak of their monthly periods as "the curse." Biblically speaking, this is somewhat correct if you include their monthly pain as preparation for childbearing.

God said that man would have to sweat for a living, and those who have cushy office jobs are recognizing that sweat is just what we need to be healthier.

C

call in question

*For we are in danger to be **called in question** for this day's uproar, there being no cause whereby we may give an account of this concourse.* (Acts 19:40)

The town clerk of Ephesus feared the town's idol makers would revolt if Paul's preaching continued because Paul was having such a devastating effect on their selling of idols: Christianity was putting the idol makers out of business.

Lawyers often call in question someone whose suspicious actions imply guilt of some kind. We also say a person that committed a wrongdoing has been "called on the carpet."

can a leopard change its spots?

*Can the Ethiopian **change** his skin, **or the leopard his spots?** then may ye also do good, that are accustomed to do evil.* (Jeremiah 13:23)

There are some people who have literally tried to change their skin color through tanning or cosmetics, but what God teaches in this verse is that man in and of himself cannot change his own nature.

The people of Judah committed so much evil that they were becoming oblivious to the fact that God would punish them. God said they could no more do good than a leopard could "change its spots."

Even though a leopard can't change its spots, a believer can get them changed. A person is said to have "spots" or blemishes if he's a sinner (2 Peter 2:13), and, of course, a sinner can have all his spots, or sins, removed by the great spot remover Himself, Jesus Christ. He leaves no stains.

can't tell whether it's coming or going

The wind bloweth where it listeth, and thou heareth the sound thereof, but <u>canst not tell whence it cometh, and whither it goeth</u>*: so is every one that is born of the Spirit.* (John 3:8)

God compared His Spirit to the wind, a very apt comparison indeed. We can't see the wind, and the same goes for God, because He and the wind He created are both invisible. The wind blows where it wants to (under God's control), and so does God's Spirit. Though we can't see the wind, we know it's there because we hear the sound and feel it on our bodies. Again, the same goes for God. Though we can't see Him, we can be sure He's there. We can feel Him in our spirit and hear Him in His words.

In this passage, Jesus spoke to Nicodemus about being born again and also compared being born again to the wind. The phrase "can't tell whether it's coming or going" refers to those who are confused or lost.

There is a connection between this original passage and today's meaning. Since this phrase was originally in the context of a lost person becoming born again, the meaning of the phrase itself of being lost is not that far removed from the biblical passage. An unbeliever does not know whether "something's coming or going" in the spiritual sense because he doesn't have his proper spiritual bearings. As the compass points to true north, so does the Bible lead us to "the Way."

cast in your lot with someone

<u>Cast in thy lot among us;</u> *let us all have one purse:* (Proverbs 1:14)

When you put in your share of the money or agree to join in on some matter, you are said to "cast in your lot." Solomon warned his son in this reference in Proverbs not to let "sinners entice thee."

When you "cast your lot" in with people, you are placing your faith and trust in them. The children of God are not supposed to be casting in their lot or placing their trust with unbelievers, for Solomon says in the next verse, "My son, walk not thou in the way with them; refrain thy foot from their path." Believers should be prepared to lose their lot, for God warned His followers several times in the Scriptures not to be "in league with" the heathen.

"Casting in your lot" is similar to gambling, for you are taking a chance and risking a lot. Gambling against God is never good odds, for He knows the "roll of the dice" anyway and sometimes causes them to roll a certain way regardless. If you want a surefire bet, cast your lot with Jesus. You won't have to worry about it being "in the cards."

cast the first stone

So when they continued asking him, he lifted up himself, and said unto them, He that is without sin among you, let him **first cast a stone** *at her.* (John 8:7)

"Casting the first stone" alludes to the famous account in the book of John about the woman caught in adultery who was brought by the Pharisees to Jesus to see what He would do with her. Jesus' answer in verse 7 ended up convicting the Pharisees, the very people that accused her. This woman was "caught in the act" (see phrase "caught in the act") as it says in verse 4 of this same chapter in John.

chosen few

For many are called, but **few** *are* **chosen**. (Matthew 22:14)

The expression "chosen few" is usually used pejoratively to mean that only a select group has been given privileges over another. When Jesus used this phrase, He meant it to show how few there are that are finally chosen by God to serve Him.

clear as day

And thine age shall be **clearer than the noonday**; *thou shalt shine forth, thou shalt be as the morning.* (Job 11:17)

Job's friend Zophar accused Job of lying about his reasons for persecution. He advised Job to put away his wickedness, and then his age would be "clearer than the noonday," differing from the present meaning of "clear as day" which signifies something that is made very understandable.

come short of

For all have sinned, and **come short of** *the glory of God.* (Romans 3:23)

"Coming short" in a matter means not quite attaining your goal, and when it comes to salvation, "almost" doesn't cut it. We all come short of God's glory and deserve a sinner's hell. However, through faith in Jesus we can have our sins forgiven. Therefore, Jesus is the only Way to salvation, and anybody that attempts another method is called a "thief" by Jesus Himself (see John 10:1). Those who try to achieve salvation by other methods will not go to heaven, for everyone needs His glory to enter into paradise according to 1 Peter 4:13–14, and 5:1.

come to pass

And now I have told you before it **come to pass**, *that, when it is* **come to pass**, *ye might believe.* (John 14:29)

One of the distinguishing characteristics of the Bible involves its use of the expression "come to pass." Jesus says in this same chapter that He was going "to prepare a place for you" (v. 2), and He continues, "And if I go and prepare a place for you, I will come again and receive you unto myself; that where I am, *there* ye may be also" (v. 3).

Many tend to forget that Jesus was also a prophet, and in this statement, he uttered a prophecy concerning what the believers had to look forward to in heaven. There really will be mansions ("In my father's house are many mansions") in heaven, so don't envy those big houses you see right now; they're nothing like what is in store for the children of God.

coming out of your ears (nose)

Ye shall not eat one day, nor two days, nor five days, neither ten days, nor twenty days; But even a whole month, until it **come out at your nostrils**, *and it be loathsome unto you: because that ye have despised the* LORD *which is among you, and have wept before him, saying, Why came we forth out of Egypt?* (Numbers 11:19–20)

To have an abundance of something or more than you can handle is to have it "coming out of your ears." God didn't take too kindly to Israel complaining about the "manna from heaven" (see **manna from heaven**) that He was sending them on a daily basis. They wanted "flesh" to eat; therefore, He told them He would give them quail, so much quail that He said it was going to "come out at your nostrils." God was going to make them sick of quail because of their constant griping about the manna. God has a way of giving people what they want and making them realize they really didn't want it to begin with.

This story should serve notice to kids who are always griping that their mothers cook the same meal all the time. Try eating fried chicken (instead of quail and manna) for thirty straight days, and you will get some idea of what the Israelites endured.

count the cost

For which of you, intending to build a tower, sitteth not down first, and **counteth the cost***, whether he have sufficient to finish it?* (Luke 14:28)

Just as a businessman has to decide if it is worth the price to begin an endeavor (i.e., "count the cost"), so also does the sinner have to count the cost and think about what it will cost him to follow Jesus. Even though salvation is free, it is at the same time the costliest thing you can obtain, for it requires the death of self, a price only a few are willing to pay.

Every sinner has to decide to lay down his life for Jesus, for "He that findeth his life shall lose it: and he that loseth his life for my sake shall find it" (Matthew 10:39). Those who know the Bible soon discover that Christianity is the exact opposite of what the world teaches. If you think Christianity's too expensive, don't buy it. It's not, however, going on sale.

cross land and sea

Woe unto you, scribes and Pharisees, hypocrites! for ye **compass sea and land** *to make one proselyte, and when he is made, ye make him twofold more the child of hell than yourselves.* (Matthew 23:15)

Jesus lashed out at His long-time enemies, the Pharisees, saying they would go to great lengths and do almost anything, i.e., "cross land and sea," to make a convert. In saying that a convert of the Pharisees was a "child of hell," Jesus, in no uncertain terms, was telling the Pharisees to their faces that they were lost. Not only did Christ say they were lost, but he also called them the children of the devil. Keep in mind that Jesus made these scathing comments to the leaders of the mainline denominations of His day. Jesus' harshest criticism was reserved for religious leaders because these were the people who should have been setting an example and will face a harsher judgment for their hypocrisy (Hebrews 13:17).

Matthew 23 shows the loving and caring Jesus calling these leaders "hypocrites," a "child of hell," "blind guides," "fools and blind," "serpents," a "generation of vipers," and "whited sepulchres." He went on to say they were "full of dead men's bones" and "full of hypocrisy and iniquity."

The world (secular and religious) tells you that this kind of name-calling is wrong, but "what saith the scriptures?" If you think name-calling is un-Christian, then why does Jesus Himself, along with Paul and many others, engage in this activity? The reason is that it is perfectly righteous to do so when justified.

cross to bear

If any man come to me, and hate not his father, and mother, and wife, and children, and brethren, and sisters, yea, and his own life also, he cannot be my disciple. And whosoever doth not **bear his cross**, *and come after me, cannot be my disciple.* (Luke 14:26–27)

This is one of the "hard sayings" of Jesus that many have difficulties with. Putting Jesus first naturally causes you to have to put family behind Him. What Jesus taught here is that if anything comes between your relationship with Him, no matter what it is, you are to forsake it, if need be, to get to Him. "Bearing your cross," or enduring hardship, is what you can expect to be the norm in your Christian walk. You as a Christian should expect an appointment with Calvary on a daily basis.

crystal clear

And he carried me away in the spirit to a great and high mountain, and shewed me that great city, the holy Jerusalem, descending out of *heaven from God, Having the glory of God; and her light was like unto a stone most precious, even like a jasper stone, **clear as crystal**.* (Revelation 21:10–11)

When you understand something very well, you are said to be "crystal clear" on the matter. What was described as "clear as crystal" in the Scriptures was the river that flowed out of the throne of Jesus in Jerusalem during Jesus' future reign on earth.

The prophet Ezekiel prophesied of this river and said it would cleanse the entire earth. Jesus will restore our planet to pristine condition. No mention is made of Jesus placing us on other planets other than the new earth He will create after destroying the old earth one thousand years after He returns. He makes that point "crystal clear" in Revelation.

cut down to the ground

*How art thou fallen from heaven, O Lucifer, son of the morning! how art thou **cut down to the ground**, which didst weaken the nations!* (Isaiah 14:12)

How appropriate that the one "cut down to the ground" in Scripture was Lucifer who lost his authority in heaven as a cherubim (angel) because of his rebellion against God. Originally, Lucifer, or Satan as he is better known, was literally "cut down to the ground" because he was in heaven and was cast down to earth. God cast out Lucifer for staging a rebellion and claiming that he would "be like the most High."

Lucifer's pride as a beautiful cherubim is the same pride that is alluded to in the phrase "cut down to the ground." We usually apply this to those whom we feel are too arrogant and who need to be brought down to earth; thus, we imply that they are so full of pride that they are up in the sky somewhere, just like Lucifer was.

cut to the quick

The God of our fathers raised up Jesus, whom ye slew and hanged on a tree. Him hath God exalted with His right hand to be a Prince and a Savior, for to give repentance to Israel, and forgiveness of sins. And we are his witnesses of these things; and so is also the Holy Ghost, whom God hath given to them that obey Him. When they heard that, they were **cut to the heart**, *and took counsel to slay them.* (Acts 5:30–33)

A Jewish council that included the high priest decided to tell the apostles not to teach in Jesus' name anymore. This same threat is repeated today when people are pressured, either directly or indirectly, to refrain from using the name "Jesus" in school graduations, public prayers, etc. Instead, they are encouraged to use the generic term, "God."

Peter's reply to these threats was that he "ought to obey God rather than men" (Acts 5:29). This is the correct thing to do when faced with the dilemma of societal and biblical laws that conflict. "Cutting to the quick," a modern equivalent of "cut to the heart" involves saying things that convict a person or upset him emotionally, or as some say, "That hit home."

D

days are numbered

So teach us to **number our days**, *that we may apply our hearts unto wisdom.* (Psalm 90:12)

Today, if an employee hears that his "days are numbered," he might want to start looking for another job, for he's on the verge of being fired.

When David implored God to "teach us to number our days," he was asking for God to help him realize that man's time on earth is short. The Scriptures teach us that we should all be living like each day could be our last. If we actually did number our days and figure out how many months and days we literally have in an average life, it might help us to put our lives in a more eternal perspective.

dead and buried

Men and brethren, let me freely speak unto you of the patriarch David, that he is both **dead and buried**, *and his sepulchre is with us unto this day.* (Acts 2:29)

Speaking on the day of Pentecost, Peter reminds the people gathered at Jerusalem that David prophesied of Jesus reigning on the throne of Jerusalem and that Jesus would be a descendant of King David who was "dead and buried." Thus, someone that is dead and buried has been dead a considerable amount of time.

Jesus' genealogical line takes up a large portion of the Bible. All those "begats" are there to prove Jesus' claim to the throne of David and to show His real descent from Adam. Those of us working on our own family trees could only hope to do as good a job as the Bible's.

dearly beloved

Dearly beloved, *avenge not yourselves, but rather give place unto wrath: for it is written, Vengeance is mine; I will repay, saith the Lord.* (Romans 12:19)

Often spoken by a preacher at weddings and funerals, the words "dearly beloved" are used by God to denote Israel and also New Testament saints, both of whom are called God's "dearly beloved."

"Dearly beloved, we are gathered here today" are the last words most people want to hear, but if it wasn't for the reality of death, how many would ever be mindful of God and the things after death? Thank God for death, for, ironically, it reminds us of eternal life. Without the death of God Himself and the shedding of His blood, nobody would have eternal life.

den of thieves

And Jesus went into the temple of God, and cast out all them that sold and bought in the temple, and overthrew the tables of the money-changers, and the seats of them that sold doves, And said unto them, It is written, My house shall be called the house of prayer; but ye have made it a **den of thieves**. (Matthew 21:13–14)

As used today, a "den of thieves" is a place where criminals gather together. It is sometimes used to describe a group of persons involved in robbery, particularly through fraud and deception.

I believe Jesus was condemning the buying and selling of items on church grounds, though others contend that He was only condemning those instances where church leaders are making a profit from God's people.

die before your time

Be not over much wicked, neither be thou foolish: why shouldest thou **die before thy time**? (Ecclesiastes 7:17)

Contrary to what many believe, it is possible to die before your time, or even to die after your time, though it is "appointed unto man once to die, and then the judgment."

Yes, each of us has an appointment with death, and it is scheduled just as precise as our next doctors' appointment; however, our appointments with death are contingent on our obedience and our fear of Him—just ask Hezekiah. God gave him an extra fifteen years because of his prayer (see Isaiah 38:5), so Hezekiah actually died after his time, but because of most people's rebellion, many will die before their time.

do as I say, not as I do

THEN spake Jesus to the multitude, and to his disciples, Saying, The scribes and the Pharisees sit in Moses' seat: All therefore whatsoever they bid you observe, that observe and do; but do not ye after their works: for **they say, and do not**. (Matthew 23:1–3)

Some of us "walk the walk," and some of us just "talk the talk," and the Pharisees and Sadducees were a prime example of how to do the latter. The Lord warned us of the "leaven of the Pharisees," this leaven being their doctrine and their hypocrisy according to Matthew 16:12 and Luke 12:1. Neither their lifestyles nor their beliefs were godly, even though the Pharisees intimidated others by their show of religion.

do unto others

And as ye would that men should do to you, **do ye also to them** *likewise.* (Luke 6:31)

One of the most famous of all biblical expressions is this one that is commonly called the "Golden Rule." Many anti-proverbs have spun off of "do unto others" such as "Do unto others before they do unto you," and "He who has the gold makes the rules."

Jesus used this proverb in His Sermon on the Mount. In His discourse, you will find many colorful expressions such as "straight and narrow," "wolf in sheep's clothing," "eye for an eye," and others that are covered in this work.

Even the unbeliever recognizes the truthfulness and practicality of "do unto others," for most everyone agrees that doing unto others as you would have them do unto you is a standard act of courtesy and behavior at home, work, or anywhere.

drink it like water

How much more abominable and filthy is man, which **drinketh iniquity like water**? (Job 15:15)

To "drink something like water" means just what it says—you drink a particular liquid as much or more than you drink water. This expression is often applied to drunkards, so the biblical context is not far removed when it speaks of those who "drinketh iniquity like water."

drop in the bucket

Behold, the nations are as a **drop of a bucket**, *and are counted as the small dust of the balance: behold, he taketh up the isles as a very little thing.* (Isaiah 40:15)

Historians like to call attention to the grandeur of empires and nations that have ruled the world at various times, but the one historian that has seen them all (i.e., God), said these nations are to Him as "a very little thing."

Such a statement by God would not be greeted warmly in a United Nations meeting. Yet compared to God's greatness, these "mighty" nations are a "drop in the bucket"—an insignificant amount compared to the whole. Seeing things through God's eyes has a way of helping you see how insignificant even the nations of the world are before Him.

E

earthshaking

Which <u>shaketh the earth</u> *out of her place, and the pillars thereof tremble.* (Job 9:6)

In the Bible, the only thing said to be earthshaking is the earth itself at the hands of God, who will shake it in the last days.

One of the signs Jesus said will occur in the last days is the predominance of earthquakes in various places. There have been more earthquakes in the last few years than at anytime since man first started recording them. The greatest earthquake in history will actually occur in the future. Revelation 16 prophesies that a great earthquake will devastate the earth just before the return of Jesus Christ.

eat, drink, and be merry

And I will say to my soul, Soul, thou hast much goods laid up for many years; take thine ease, <u>eat, drink, and be merry</u>. (Luke 12:19)

The reigning philosophy of the heathen is exemplified in this very popular expression whose modern counterpart is "sex, drugs, and rock-n-roll." The biblical context involves the parable of the rich man who had to build bigger barns to store his goods, and after doing so, decided it was time to relax and "eat, drink, and be merry."

Being happy or merry is the purpose of life for millions, including those who profess to know Jesus, but being happy should not be their primary goal. Glorifying God and enjoying Him is the purpose for our creation according to Revelation 4:11. As every

Christian knows, happiness comes as a result of a right relationship with God.

eat one's words

Thy <u>words</u> *were found, and I did* <u>eat them</u>*; and thy word was unto me the joy and rejoicing of mine heart: for I am called by thy name, O* LORD *God of hosts.* (Jeremiah 15:16)

When you make a statement to others that you might regret later, you might have to "eat your words." As far as God is concerned, He would love for you to eat His words, for the psalmist says that His words are "sweeter than honey, and the honeycomb" (Psalm 19:10).

eats me up

For the zeal of thine house hath <u>eaten me up</u>*; and the reproaches of them that reproached thee are fallen upon me.* (Psalm 69:9)

David prophesied of Jesus' ministry on earth and one of the chief characteristics of that ministry. What ate Jesus up inside was the zeal that he had for the house of God (see **den of thieves**). Being called a "zealot" these days carries with it negative connotations; nonetheless, Jesus could rightfully be considered a "zealot."

A modern equivalent of the word "zealot" would be "fanatic." Of course, the world seems to think it is okay to be a fanatic about anything except God. Those who are zealous for God and live righteously are often labeled "religious fanatics" and seen as "extremists," terms that are thrown around by those who want everyone to be "middle-of-the-roaders." Jesus Christ, our perfect example, was certainly an "extremist." When He says, "I am the way, the truth, and the life" (John 14:6), He leaves no room for moderation.

eleventh hour

And when they came that were hired about **the eleventh hour,** *they received every man a penny.* (Matthew 20:9)

"The eleventh hour" signifies the time that is left just before a deadline. Jesus applied the term in His parable of the laborers by telling of "eleventh hour" or last minute laborers who were hired by a farmer but who were paid the same wages as the helpers that had worked all day.

end is near

They hunt our steps, that we cannot go in our streets: our **end is near,** *our days are fulfilled; for our end is come.* (Lamentations 4:18)

Just the mention of this phrase conjures up images of the proverbial man with the sandwich boards walking down the street with the words "The end is near" on his front and backside.

As used in this verse, the statement "end is near" refers to Israel's complaints against her enemies and her fear that the nation itself was in jeopardy. Today, it's not hard to see the signs of the times (see **signs of the times**) and know that "the end is near," the phrase itself being an allusion to the Second Coming of Jesus and the end of time.

end of the world

Teaching them to observe all things whatsoever I have commanded you: and, lo, I am with you alway, even unto **the end of the world.** *Amen.* (Matthew 28:20)

"Hey, it's not the end of the world," people will say when trying to comfort themselves or someone else.

According to Scripture, the world will not end until after Armageddon and the return of Jesus. At that time, Jesus will make a "new heaven and a new earth" (Revelation 21:1). Christians truly can take comfort in the presence of Christ, even when their circumstances make them feel like their world is coming to an end.

ends of the earth

For so hath the Lord commanded us, saying, I have set thee to be a light of the Gentiles, that thou shouldest be for salvation unto **the ends of the earth**. (Acts 13:47)

Anyone that will go to great lengths to help you or that will go anywhere to assist you could be described as going to "the ends of the earth" for you. As used here in a quote from Isaiah 49:6, God's people are commanded to testify for Him to the far corners of our planet.

error of one's ways

Brethren, if any of you do err from the truth, and one convert him; Let him know, that he which converteth the sinner from the **error of his way** *shall save a soul from death, and shall hide a multitude of sins.* (James 5:19–20)

Today, when people are confronted about their mistaken beliefs or wicked acts and those some people react by correcting their beliefs or actions, they are said to have seen "the error of their ways."

In these verses, James instructs his readers that to truly be converted from the error of one's ways, one must come to the knowledge of the truth. Forgiveness in Christ is the only way to save one's soul from eternal death, and His atonement is the only way to cover our sin.

evil eye

Eat thou not the bread of him that hath an **evil eye**, *neither desire thou his dainty meats:* (Proverbs 23:6)

You can always tell the bad guy in the movies—he's the one with the evil eye or the sinister look. Solomon, the king of Israel, talks about this evil-eyed person in the Proverbs.

It is interesting that in the next verse, this person with the evil eye is also the subject of another famous quote: "For as a man thinks in his heart, so he is." The text actually says, "as he thinketh," speaking specifically of the evil-eyed person just mentioned.

The eyes tell us a lot about a person, as Jesus Himself testified in Matthew 6:22: "The light of the body is the eye: if therefore thine eye be single, thy whole body shall be full of light." Evil is reflected in one's eyes, so don't wonder why some people won't look you in the eye.

eye for an eye

Ye have heard that it hath been said, An **eye for an eye**, *and a tooth for a tooth:* (Matthew 5:38)

Possibly the best known of biblical expressions is this one that Jesus quotes from the Old Testament (Exodus 21:24). Contrary to popular opinion, these verses do not give anyone the right of personal vengeance. According to Exodus 21, "an eye for an eye" was the method a judge would use to determine the proper punishment for a crime; thus, the punishment would fit the crime.

F

face-to-face

And Jacob called the name of the place Peniel: for I have seen God **face to face***, and my life is preserved.* (Genesis 32:30)

Each one of us, like Jacob, will have a face-to-face meeting with the God of this universe, for God says "that at the name of Jesus every knee should bow" and also "*that* every tongue should confess that Jesus Christ *is* Lord." Our knees will not bow because we are forced to but because the sheer greatness of Jesus Himself will prompt us to fall to the ground and worship. It will be like the scarecrow meeting the Wizard of Oz—only multiply that experience times ten thousand.

We are not meeting some ambiguous spirit; we will actually see the face of God, Jesus Christ, who "is the image of the invisible God" (Colossians 1:15).

fall by the wayside

And when he sowed, some seeds **fell by the way side***, and the fowls came, and devoured them up:* (Matthew 13:4)

In His parable of the sower, Jesus described four kinds of soil in which a certain planter planted his seeds, the seeds representing the word of God, and the different soils representing the various hearers of the word. One type of soil ultimately became productive, but the others did not. The seed that the Bible says "fell by the wayside" corresponds to those who are influenced by the word of God, but has that influence taken away by Satan before they can trust in Christ.

"Falling by the wayside" speaks of something that has gone into disservice or neglect or of someone that has just dropped out of society (cf. Matthew 20:30; Luke 18:35). Spiritually speaking, "falling by the wayside" takes on a far more serious note, signifying the seeds of those who don't get "planted" correctly.

fall from grace

Christ is become of no effect unto you, whosoever of you are justified by the law; ye are **fallen from grace**. (Galatians 5:4)

Paul here blasts the notion that a Christian has to earn his way to heaven by good works. Those who believe this, he says, have "fallen from grace," meaning they are no longer living by the grace of God.

Today, the meaning of this phrase has shifted somewhat to include falling out of favor or losing one's position in any endeavor. If people believe God weighs their good and bad deeds and passes judgment accordingly, they miss the whole reason that God had to save mankind in the first place—because their evil hearts prevent them from saving themselves through good works.

fall into the hands of ...

It is a fearful thing to **fall into the hands of** *the living God.* (Hebrews 10:31)

Sometimes things are said to have "fallen into the wrong hands" if they end up in the possession of an undesirable person. In this verse, falling into the hands of the living God is equivalent to falling under the judgment of God. This dreadful fate awaits all who have not repented and been redeemed through Christ.

fall on your sword

*And when his armourbearer saw that Saul was dead, he **fell** likewise **up**on his **sword**, and died with him.* (1 Samuel 31:5)

King Saul committed suicide after realizing that he was going to lose his battle against the Philistines, and upon seeing Saul's demise, his armor bearer did the same.

"Shooting yourself in the foot" would be a close equivalent of this biblical expression found in the book of Samuel. This saying is another example of a literal expression of the Bible being turned into a metaphorical one for today.

far be it from me

*And Joab answered and said, Far be it, **far be it from me**, that I should swallow up or destroy.* (2 Samuel 20:20)

An equivalent expression might be, "I wouldn't dream of doing such a thing." Joab, one of David's officers in his army, was pursuing a man named Sheba who took up arms against David. Joab followed him to a certain city and told that city's leader that he wanted only Sheba, not the city. Speaking of the city, he said, "Far be it from me that I should swallow up or destroy."

fear of God (put the fear of God into someone)

*And **the fear of God** was on all the kingdoms of those countries, when they had heard that the LORD had fought against the enemies of Israel.* (2 Chronicles 20:29)

The fact that Israel even exists is a modern miracle. She is surrounded by enemies that have waged war constantly to destroy her, but God has protected her as He promised He would. He has done this by "putting the fear of God" into all those countries who fight and try unsuccessfully to defeat her.

The expression is used today to describe extreme fear and is often attributed to the actions of an individual, "He really put the fear of God into them." The true fear of God is so awesome that those who are affected by it either run to God in faith or, as in Revelation 6:16, try desperately to hide themselves.

feet of clay

*His legs of iron, his **feet** part of iron and part **of clay**.* (Daniel 2:33)

When you learn about a particular fault someone has that you didn't suspect he or she had, this person is said to have "feet of clay"—an undetected weakness. As used in the book of Daniel, "feet of clay" makes reference to the feet of an idol that Daniel saw in a vision.

According to the Bible's own interpretation of the vision, certain parts of the idol's body in Daniel's vision each represented kingdoms that were to rule the world. The image's feet stood for the fourth and last kingdom described as "part of iron and part of clay." Some have equated this kingdom with the kingdom of Antichrist. Though many during this time will worship the Antichrist and consider him to be perfect, Almighty God will reveal his inherent weakness, conquering him and his forces and establishing Christ's earthly kingdom.

fight like a man

*Be strong, and quit yourselves like men, O ye Philistines, that ye be not servants unto the Hebrews, as they have been to you: **quit yourselves like men, and fight**.* (1 Samuel 4:9)

In this day of women's rights and the feminist movement, phrases like this may not go over too well with the "modern woman." Even so, when was the last time you heard someone encouraged to "fight like a woman."

The Philistines were battling Israel and exhorted each other to "fight like men" after some of their men had expressed fear on account of how Israel had conquered other armies with the famous Ark of the Covenant.

It must be remembered that the exhortation to "fight like a man" was not given by God but rather by the Philistines. God, on the other hand, exhorts people to fight the good fight (see the next entry).

fight the good fight

Fight the good fight *of faith, lay hold on eternal life, whereunto thou art also called, and hast professed a good profession before many witnesses.* (1 Timothy 6:12)

To "fight the good fight" involves being aggressive in defending a good cause. Paul is reminding his young disciple Timothy that to be a good Christian, Timothy has to be like a soldier in a war, because the true Christian is fighting a real war with real enemies. Paul further defines this fight as a fight to keep the faith (2 Timothy 4:7).

filthy rich (lucre)

*A bishop then must be blameless, the husband of one wife, vigilant, sober, of good behavior, given to hospitality, apt to teach; Not given to wine, no striker, not greedy of **filthy lucre**; but patient, not a brawler, not covetous;* (1 Timothy 3:3)

"Filthy rich" and "filthy lucre" both refer to money gotten illegally or immorally. In the Scriptures, this phrase makes reference to false teachers and preachers who teach "for filthy lucre's sake," that is, just for the money.

finger of God

Then the magicians said unto Pharaoh, This is **the finger of God***: and Pharaoh's heart was hardened, and he hearkened not unto them; as the* LORD *had said.* (Exodus 8:19)

People will usually proclaim God had something to do with a situation when something miraculous seemingly happens. They will then cry out that "the finger of God" is present.

Pharaoh's magicians cried out this same thing when God turned the dust of the ground into lice and plagued Egypt for not letting the Hebrew slaves go free. The magicians had apparently duplicated God's acts of bringing frogs out of the water and turning the water into blood, but they could not duplicate the lice being brought from the dust.

Even Pharaoh's magicians recognized God's hand in the matter by proclaiming it to be the "finger of God," though Pharaoh refused to do as they suggested. God gets even His enemies to proclaim His mighty acts.

fire and brimstone

But the fearful, and unbelieving, and the abominable, and murderers, and whoremongers, and sorcerers, and idolaters, and all liars, shall have their part in the lake which burneth with **fire and brimstone***: which is the second death.* (Revelation 21:8)

Those who often preach on hell and the lake of fire are labeled "fire and brimstone" preachers and are relegated as too harsh and unloving by much of modern man. Yet Jesus Himself spoke much more of hell than He did of heaven.

In Mark 9, Jesus told the same people three times that hell awaited those who rejected God, saying that hell is "where worm dieth not, and the fire is not quenched." In 2 Thessalonians 1:8, Paul spoke of God's wrath being poured out on the heathen: "In flaming fire taking vengeance on them that know not God, and that obey not the gospel of our Lord Jesus Christ."

fire in his eyes

His head and his hairs were white like wool, as white as snow; and his <u>*eyes were as a flame of fire*</u>*;* (Revelation 1:14)

Guess who has fire in His eyes in the Bible? It was the loving, caring Jesus according to the apostle John's vision of Jesus in the book of Revelation. To have "fire in your eyes" means you are extremely angry, and this usage is connected in meaning with the biblical context where Jesus is described as having eyes "as a flame of fire."

It is seldom taught today that God is angry with anyone, but the Bible declares otherwise in Psalm 2, where it says God "is angry with the wicked every day." Jesus is so angry with the wicked that at the Great White Throne He will literally cast millions into hell.

flesh and blood

And Jesus answered and said unto him, Blessed art thou Simon Bar-jona: for <u>*flesh and blood*</u> *hath not revealed it unto thee, but my Father which is in heaven.* (Matthew 16:17)

Your own "flesh and blood" is another way of saying your children, parents, relatives, or people in general. Jesus employed the term after Peter acknowledged that Jesus was "the Christ, the son of the living God." Peter's statement that Jesus was "the Son of the living God" was not revealed to him by "flesh and blood"—in other words, man, but by God Himself.

fly in the ointment

*Dead **flies** cause **the ointment** of the apothecary to send forth a stinking savor: so doth a little folly him that is in reputation for wisdom and honour.* (Ecclesiastes 10:1)

Just as a fly in the soup ruins a meal, so does a fly in the ointment ruin a jar of salve! As it is used in this verse of Scripture, the "fly in the ointment" is likened to the ruining of a good man's reputation. When he commits a "little folly." A wise man will shun foolishness and folly for this very reason.

follow in the steps of . . .

*For even hereunto were ye called: because Christ also suffered for us, leaving us an example, that ye should **follow his steps**:* (1 Peter 2:21)

How appropriate that the person we are to "follow in the footsteps of," or emulate, according to scripture, is Jesus Christ Himself. Following anyone else could lead you to idolatry, which is often masqueraded in the heroes and role models of today. If you want to play "follow the leader," follow the true one, Jesus Christ, and you will never be disappointed.

for Christ's sake

*We are fools **for Christ's sake**, but ye are wise in Christ; we are weak, but ye are strong; ye are honorable, but we are despised.* (1 Corinthians 4:10)

To utter "for Christ's sake" is to implore someone or to express unbelief or amazement. Its usage in the Bible is literal, as opposed to the modern, euphemistic counterpart. "We are fools," Paul said, "for Christ's sake," speaking of the apostles' persecution and their being "appointed to death."

four corners of the earth

*AND after these things I saw four angels standing on **the four corners of the earth**, holding the four winds of the earth, that the wind should not blow on the earth, nor on the sea, nor on any tree.* (Revelation 7:1)

The phrase "the four corners of the earth" as we use it today speaks of far away places. The same Greek phrase is translated "four quarters of the earth" in Revelation 20:18. It seems to be used to describe the entire world.

from time to time

*And thy meat which thou shalt eat shall be by weight, twenty shekels a day: **from time to time** shalt thou eat it.* (Ezekiel 4:10)

God sometimes told men to do some strange things in the Bible, and these instructions to Ezekiel are a prime example. God instructed the prophet to lie on his side 390 consecutive days, each day to represent a year of Israel's iniquity. While lying on his side, Ezekiel was to eat meat and drink "from time to time."

fruits of your labor

*But if I live in the flesh, this is the **fruit of my labor**: yet what I shall choose I wot not.* (Philippians 1:22)

To see the results of your work is to realize and enjoy the "fruits of your labor." Paul's labor was preaching the gospel, and he saw the results of his work with his converts that he was helping to grow in the faith.

Notice that fruit is the result of labor, or work. Any gardener knows the incredible amount of time and labor it takes to grow a fruit, and as it grows, the effort at protecting it from bugs, birds, and diseases is a job in itself.

fuel to the fire

Thou shalt be for __fuel to the fire__*; thy blood shall be in the midst of the land; thou shalt be no more remembered: for I the* Lord *have spoken it.* (Ezekiel 21:32)

Don't "add fuel to the fire" we are told when we make a bad situation worse or keep a conflict going. God prophesies of His judgment of the Ammonites for their lying and vanity against Israel. Because of this, He says that the Ammonites will be "fuel to the fire."

G

get your house in order

IN those days was Hezekiah sick unto death. And the prophet Isaiah the son of Amoz came to him, and said unto him, Thus saith the LORD, **Set thine house in order;** *for thou shalt die, and not live.* (2 Kings 20:1)

God told King Hezekiah, "Set thine house in order" because the king was going to die. God, however, extended his life by fifteen years on account of the king's fervent prayer. We usually hear this expression when something serious is going on (like a life-threatening illness), and we need to have ourselves prepared and organized.

give credit where credit is due

Render therefore to all their dues: **tribute to whom tribute is due;** *custom to whom custom; fear to whom fear; honor to whom honor.* (Romans 13:7)

When Jesus was asked about paying taxes, His reply was to "Render therefore unto Caesar the things which are Caesar's." Need the Bible remind you, those to whom we are to pay taxes are called God's ministers. Of course, if they owe us money, then they need to give credit where credit is due, or as the Bible says, "tribute to whom tribute is due."

Acknowledging someone's accomplishments is the meaning of "giving credit where credit is due." Acknowledging the IRS as God's ministers, though not an easy task, is something that might make it easier to pay those taxes come April 15th.

give up the ghost

*Then Abraham **gave up the ghost**, and died in a good old age, an old man, and full of years; and was gathered to his people.* (Genesis 25:8)

Though the expression "gave up the ghost" is used as a delicate way of saying that someone has died, it happens to be an accurate account of what occurs at death. When an individual dies, the Bible says the spirit, or ghost, returns "unto God who gave it" (Ecclesiastes 12:7).

gnash your teeth

*But the children of the kingdom shall be cast out into outer darkness: there shall be weeping and **gnashing of teeth**.* (Matthew 8:12)

This phrase can be used to describe someone in great anger or great pain. Jesus uses it here to describe the feeling experienced by those cast into hell. The wicked quite often gnash their teeth in Scripture. In this verse, Christ describes the emotional state of the wicked once they realize it is too late to decide to go through the narrow gate and live in the straight way.

God bless you

*The **Lord bless thee**, and keep thee.* (Numbers 6:24)

Just because God blesses you, don't get the notion that all is well. Throughout Scripture, God at times blesses even the heathen. Even though God does bless us with many wonderful things, let us not forget that He also curses those who are against Him (see Genesis 12:3).

God forbid

What then? shall we sin, because we are not under the law, but under grace? **God forbid.** (Romans 6:15)

Speaking to the church at Rome, Paul tried to dispel the notion that Christians could continue in sin because they weren't "under the law, but under grace." Paul's reaction was a resounding "No," or "God forbid." The doctrine of salvation by grace in no way gives the believer a license to indulge his wicked desires.

The phrase in the Greek actually means "may it never be." The translators of the King James Version of the Bible, in order to show the extreme negation intended in the phrase, translated it "God forbid." A similar phrase is used in the Old Testament (Joshua 22:29), and it is highly likely that Paul's familiarity with the Old Testament phrase led him to use the equivalent Greek phrase throughout the book of Romans.

God is my witness

For **God is my witness,** *whom I serve with my spirit in the gospel of his Son, that without ceasing I make mention of you always in my prayers.* (Romans 1:9)

There has been an eyewitness to every crime ever committed over the history of time, and that witness is Jesus Christ. Just think if you had access to view every crime committed in every second of every day. God has this access, for "The eyes of the LORD *are* in every place, beholding the evil and the good" (Proverbs 15:3). The phrase is used today as an exclamation of one's own veracity. Even if some can't prove what they are saying is true, they will declare that God is a witness to the truth of what they are proclaiming.

God save the king!

And it came to pass, when Hushai the Archite, David's friend, was come unto Absalom, that Hushai said unto Absalom, **God save the king, God save the king***.* (2 Samuel 16:16)

No English king is crowned without hearing the familiar proclamation, "God save the king!" Hushai, a friend of King David, also proclaimed these very words when he met David's son Absalom. Absalom didn't want God to save the king; instead, he wanted to overthrow his father David.

Kings and rulers around the world don't get the respect and honor they deserve despite the Scriptures' clear admonitions for their honor: "Fear God. Honor the king" (1 Peter 2:17). When the King of kings reigns supreme in Jerusalem, He will get respect, and He will not share His power with anyone.

good for nothing

Ye are the salt of the earth: but if the salt have lost his savor, wherewith shall it be salted? it is thenceforth **good for nothing***, but to be cast out, and to be trodden under foot of men.* (Matthew 5:13)

Christians should take heed at this warning given by Jesus in His preaching to the multitudes. If a Christian has lost his testimony or zeal for God, he is not fit to do anything in this world and will end up a reject. He will not be useful for the world, the church, or God; thus, he will be "good for nothing."

Trying to please the world and God not only is wicked and worthless (good for nothing), but also will get you "trodden under foot of men," or "stepped all over" as the world would say.

good Lord

For a multitude of the people, even many of Ephraim, and Manasseh, Issachar, and Zebulun, had not cleansed themselves, yet did they eat the passover otherwise than it was written. But Hezekiah prayed for them, saying, **The good LORD** *pardon every one That prepareth his heart to seek God, the* LORD *God of his fathers, though he be not cleansed according to the purification of the sanctuary.* (2 Chronicles 30:18–19)

As used here and in Christian society, this phrase is a common title used of God and particularly of Jesus. It is often used to describe God as a giver of blessings and mercy. In slang, "good lord" is used as an expression of disdain, usually directed toward someone or some event that does not live up to that person's expectations.

good name

A GOOD name *is rather to be chosen than great riches, and loving favour rather than silver and gold.* (Proverbs 22:1)

A good name "is better than precious ointment" according to Ecclesiastes 7:1. When a person has a good name in the community, he usually is considered a person of integrity. However, beware "when all men speak well of you," as Jesus said, "for so did the fathers to the false prophets."

Having a good name is not the same as having everyone like you. You will likely have many enemies if you are living the life of a Christian, but righteous living can keep you a good name, even among your enemies. Trying to make everyone like you is not the job of a Christian. A Christian with no enemies is not living for God, just for his supposed good name.

goodness' sake

Remember not the sins of my youth, nor my transgressions: according to thy mercy remember thou me **for thy goodness' sake***, O* LORD. (Psalm 25:7)

Often used as a substitute for "heaven's sake," or "for Christ's sake," the phrase "for goodness' sake" is a convenient euphemism for those who are slightly conscientious of using God's name in vain. David speaks in this passage of Scripture and asks God to forget "the sins of my youth" in order to show "thy goodness' sake."

God does everything He does for His "goodness' sake," not ours. He created everything for His pleasure, not ours. He didn't create the universe because He needed someone to show His love to, but rather because He wanted to make His glory known throughout His creation. That is heresy. God needs nothing, and that includes us. He is perfect and complete in all His ways, and out of His sheer mercy we are brought into a saving knowledge of Him.

go on all fours

Whatsoever goeth upon the belly, and whatsoever **goeth upon all four**, *or whatsoever hath more feet among all creeping things that creep upon the earth, them ye shall not eat for they are an abomination.* (Leviticus 11:42)

In this verse, God explains to Moses and Aaron the difference between clean and unclean things as it related to the Hebrew dietary law. The Jews, as most know, abstain from eating certain foods like pork, fish without scales, or meat with blood in it. Today, to "go on all fours" is to act like an animal.

go the extra mile

And whosoever shall compel thee to **go a mile, go with him twain**. (Matthew 5:41)

Jesus, the original proponent of going the extra mile, taught His disciples to do the same. Literally, He instructs us to do at least twice as much as is asked of us. The teaching and lesson here is to do more than we're expected to do.

go the way of all flesh

I **go the way of all the earth**: *be thou strong therefore, and shew thyself a man;* (1 Kings 2:2)

The only sure things according to this world are said to be death and taxes. The only exception to this rule (as far as death is concerned) is Enoch and Elijah, who escaped death and were taken up into heaven. As King David lay dying, he tried to encourage Solomon to be strong. In the verses that follow, he directed Solomon to follow after the Lord and keep His commandments.

go through fire and water

Thou hast caused men to ride over our heads; we **went through fire and through water**: *but thou broughtest us out into a wealthy place.* (Psalm 66:12)

This expression speaks of going to great lengths and striving diligently for someone or something. The Israelites made reference to this phrase but meant it literally when they mentioned going through the Red Sea's wall of water and the "pillar of fire" that protected them from the Egyptians.

The history of God's judgments on earth can also be summed up as going through fire and water. Noah's flood was the water judgment, and fire is the next: "Whereby the world that then was, being overflowed with water, perished: But the heavens and the earth, which are now, by the same word are kept in store, reserved unto fire against the day of judgment and perdition of ungodly men" (2 Peter 6–7). God has no intention of saving this earth for anyone; He's going to make a new one that's even better.

greener pastures

He maketh me to lie down in **green pastures**: *he leadeth me beside the still waters.* (Psalm 23:2)

People are always looking for something better or newer, whether it be a mate, a job, a car, etc. "If I could just get such and such, I'd be happy" is a lie because the Bible says, "The eyes of man are never satisfied." If you really want to find greener pastures, seek after God, not the things of this world, and He will lead you to them.

half dead

And Jesus answering said, A certain man went down from Jerusalem to Jericho, and fell among thieves, which stripped him of his raiment, and wounded him, and departed, leaving him **half dead**. (Luke 10:30)

The story of the Good Samaritan is familiar to most everyone. The man that the Samaritan helped had been robbed and hurt and was literally "half dead." Saying you're "half dead" today means you're extremely exhausted.

half was not told me

Howbeit I believed not the words, until I came, and mine eyes had seen it: and, behold, **the half was not told me**: *thy wisdom and prosperity exceedeth the fame which I heard.* (1 Kings 10:7)

"You haven't heard the half of it" is the expression we might use to describe a situation that has a lot of details yet to be revealed. This biblical context involved the Queen of Sheba's visit to King Solomon.

According to Jesus, King Solomon was the wisest man to ever live. Solomon got this wisdom from his prayer to God at the dedication of the Jewish Temple that the king had built. When God asked him to name what he wanted, Solomon asked for wisdom.

hand in hand

Though **hand join in hand**, *the wicked shall not be unpunished: but the seed of the righteous shall be delivered.* (Proverbs 11:21)

"Hand in hand" has come to be associated with lovers walking and holding hands or two people working closely together in agreement. The biblical usage refers to the wicked who unite "hand in hand" to accomplish some supposed great feat. Their unity does not impress God, who says that in spite of their great deeds, they will not go unpunished.

hardheaded

As an adamant **harder** *than flint have I made thy fore***head***: fear them not, neither be dismayed at their looks, though they be a rebellious house.* (Ezekiel 3:9)

Because Israel would not listen to God, God chose Ezekiel the prophet to speak unto them. He made the prophet's head "harder than flint" so that Ezekiel would not fear or "be dismayed at their looks." Being called "hardheaded" today means you have the reputation of not changing your mind in the face of other viewpoints. Being hardheaded for God means you don't compromise your position or belief in the face of adversity.

heart and soul

Jesus said unto him, Thou shalt love the Lord thy God with all thy **heart, and** *with all thy* **soul***, and with all thy mind. This is the first and great commandment* (Matthew 22:37–38)

Devoting all of yourself and your efforts to accomplish something is the meaning of this biblical expression. According to Jesus and the Old Testament, loving God has to be done with heart and soul in order to obey the greatest commandment of all. It's all or nothing with God as far as your heart is concerned, so "set your heart" on Him, and He will give you your "heart's desire."

heart of stone

And I will give them one heart, and I will put a new spirit within you; and I will take the **stony heart** *out of their flesh, and will give them an heart of flesh.* (Ezekiel 11:19)

"He has a good heart," some people will say, or "His heart is in the right place." Since God looks upon the heart and not the outward appearance, His opinion may be quite different from the norm. Everyone without God has a heart of stone and needs a new heart.

hearts and minds

And the peace of God, which passeth all understanding, shall keep your **hearts and minds** *through Christ Jesus.* (Philippians 4:7)

We speak of someone winning "the hearts and minds" of another group of people when a leader or influential person gets the affections and approval of his followers. For a Christian, the peace of God keeps their "hearts and minds through Christ Jesus." The peace of mind that everyone is looking for comes only from Jesus. Peace in anything else is a false sense of security.

heart's desire

BRETHREN, my **heart's desire** *and prayer to God for Israel is, that they might be saved.* (Romans 10:1)

That which one wants above all else is an apt description of the expression "heart's desire," and what Paul wanted most was for the Jews to be saved.

In considering these things, one must remember the admonition of Jesus, "For where your treasure is, there will your heart be also" (Matthew 6:21).

heat of the day

And when they had received it, they murmered against the goodman of the house, Saying, These last have wrought but one hour, and thou hast made them equal unto us, which have borne the burden and **heat of the day**. (Matthew 20:11–12)

The hottest part of the day, or "heat of the day," is not something most office workers with all of their air-conditioned comfort ever experience. Most people don't really have to work by the sweat of their brow anymore. The closest some of us get to sweating everyday is when we get in our car and it hasn't cooled off sufficiently yet.

heavy handed

For day and night thy **hand was heavy** *upon me: my moisture is turned into the drought of summer. Selah.* (Psalm 32:4)

A "heavy handed" person is someone who is overly dramatic and harsh. David mentioned how God's hand was heavy upon him. David is speaking of a time when he failed to acknowledge his sin before God. As David confesses his guilt and seeks forgiveness from God, his sorrow is turned to gladness.

heavy heart

As he that taketh away a garment in cold weather, and as vinegar upon nitre, so is he that singeth songs to **an heavy heart**. (Proverbs 25:20)

A heart that is weighed down with despair or trouble can be called a "heavy heart." This passage from Proverbs warns not to try to force a heavy-hearted person to be cheerful by singing lyrical, joyful music to them. To act with such disregard to one's sorrow is likened to taking a vagrant's garment from him in the winter.

here a little and there a little

For precept must be upon precept, precept upon precept; line upon line, line upon line; <u>*here a little, and there a little*</u>*:* (Isaiah 28:10)

When a person speaks of the knowledge he has gained over the years, he sometimes refers to acquiring it "here a little, and there a little."

Just like a baby must be weaned from his mother's milk, so the believer must be weaned from the "milk of the word" before he or she can have the "strong meat" the Bible contains.

here and there

And as thy servant was busy <u>*here and there,*</u> *he was gone. And the king of Israel said unto him, So shall thy judgment be; thyself hast decided it.* (1 Kings 20:40)

"Here and there" means various places, and its biblical usage hasn't changed. "Here and there" is the equivalent of "hither and thither," an expression that is also used in the Bible (2 Kings 2:8, 14).

here today and gone tomorrow

Wherefore, if God so clothe the grass of the field, **which** <u>**to day is, and to morrow is cast into the oven**</u>*, shall he not much more clothe you, O ye of little faith?* (Matthew 6:30)

We usually speak of something that doesn't last long as "fly by night" or "here today, gone tomorrow." The expression is also used for individuals who are unreliable and unpredictable. "Here today and gone tomorrow" is especially relevant in these fast moving times where people and businesses are constantly moving.

Though all else is transient, Hebrews 13:8 says that Jesus Christ is "the same yesterday, and to day, and for ever." His words are just as sure as it states in Isaiah: "The grass withereth, the flower fadeth: but the word of our God shall stand for ever" (Isaiah 40:8).

he thinks he's something

For if <u>a man think himself to be something,</u> *when he is nothing, he deceiveth himself.* (Galatians 6:3)

We've all heard people describe someone they think is arrogant by saying, "He thinks he's really something." God said if you think you're "something" when you're actually nothing, you are deceived.

Paul mentioned that we ought not to think more highly of ourselves than we should (Romans 12:3). And John the Baptist said of Jesus, "He must increase, but I *must* decrease" (John 3:30). Our goal should be for us to become "nothing" and Jesus to become everything.

high-handed

And the LORD hardened the heart of Pharaoh king of Egypt, and he pursued after the children of Israel: and the children of Israel went out with an <u>high hand.</u> (Exodus 14:8)

To be high-handed is to be inconsiderate of others or not to consult others before doing something. The "high hand" that the children of Israel went out with, however, is merely a symbol of the might of Israel, due to the nation's deliverance by God. The modern and biblical usages are somewhat connected. Those who attribute their might to themselves rather than to God will be inconsiderate of the feelings and opinions of others.

high heaven

It is as **high** as **heaven**; *what canst thou do? deeper than hell; what canst thou know?* (Job 11:8)

"That stinks to high heaven," is a common use of this expression and means that something stinks so bad, it can be smelled all the way to heaven. According to Job's friend, Zophar, the knowledge of God reaches past the heights of heaven and below the depths of hell.

high noon

And he said, Lo, it is yet **high day**, *neither is it time that the cattle should be gathered together: water ye the sheep, and go and feed them.* (Genesis 29:7)

"High noon" can mean exactly noon or refer to the apex or pinnacle of a person's endeavors. Although it is designated "high day" in Genesis, the sense is still the same. The phrase derives from the position of the sun in the sky, which is highest at noon.

his highness

For destruction from God was a terror to me, and by reason of **his highness** *I could not endure.* (Job 31:23)

This expression is often used derisively for someone who acts "high and mighty," but who really isn't. Job used it literally and spoke of how he couldn't fight against God and "His Highness," that is, His power and greatness. Job realized that he could only "win by losing" as Jesus later said: "He that loseth his life for my sake shall find it" (Matthew 10:39).

hold my tongue

Thou art of purer eyes than to behold evil, and canst not look on iniq-
uity: wherefore lookest thou upon them that deal treacherously, and
<u>holdest thy tongue</u> *when the wicked devoureth the man that is more*
righteous than he? (Habakkuk 1:13)

The prophet Habakkuk, along with countless others, wants to
know why God "holds His tongue," or doesn't say anything, about
the many evils that befall righteous people.

Man usually blames everything but his own evil heart for his
problems. Yet Jesus Himself said in Matthew 15:19: "For out of
the heart proceed evil thoughts, murders, adulteries, fornications,
thefts, false witness, blasphemies: These are the things which defile
a man: but to eat with unwashen hands defileth not a man."

holier than thou

Which say, Stand by thyself, come not near to me; for I am <u>holier than</u>
<u>thou</u>. *These are a smoke in my nose, a fire that burneth all the day.*
(Isaiah 65:5)

God accused the self-righteous Israelites of being holier-than-
thou because they thought they were so much better than others
that they didn't want others coming near them. God also said this
attitude was a "smoke in my nose."

Today, "holier-than-thou" is used derisively of those who act
or seem to think they are better than anyone else.

Holy Land

And the Lord shall inherit Judah his portion in <u>the holy land,</u> *and shall*
choose Jerusalem again. (Zechariah 2:3)

The land of Israel, because it was set apart by God, is referred
to as the Holy Land. Jesus Himself will rule there after His tri-
umphant return.

Holy of Holies

And after the second veil, the tabernacle which is called **the Holiest of all.** (Hebrews 9:3)

The world has taken this phrase and applied it to any secret chamber, special place of reverence, or other area deemed "off limits." In the Scriptures, it refers to the inner chamber of the tabernacle, and later, the temple. Only the high priest could enter the Holy of Holies, once a year on the Day of Atonement. The veil that separated the Holy of Holies in Herod's Temple was rent in half when Christ died on the cross, signifying that the way of salvation through Christ was open to all.

holy water

And the priest shall take **holy water** *in an earthen vessel; and of the dust that is in the floor of the tabernacle the priest shall take, and put it into the water.* (Numbers 5:17)

God did say the Jews had "holy water" to use for special occasions, but this referred to ordinary water that was set apart for a particular purpose. Today's use of holy water is another instance of trying to ascribe some mystical power to a part of God's creation.

hope against hope

Who **against hope believed in hope,** *that he might become the father of many nations; according to that which was spoken, So shall thy seed be.* (Romans 4:18)

To "hope against hope" is to believe, like Abraham, that something hoped for will come to pass even when there seems to be no chance that it will. Abraham believed that his wife would have a child at one hundred years of age and that this child's descendants would eventually produce the Messiah, Jesus Christ.

"Hoping against hope" is comparable to believing in something when others are saying, "You don't have a prayer."

house divided against itself

And Jesus knew their thoughts, and said unto them, Every kingdom divided against itself is brought to desolation; and every city or **house divided against itself** *shall not stand:* (Matthew 12:25)

Known for its usage in Lincoln's famous Civil War speech, the expression "house divided against itself" comes from this passage in Matthew in which Jesus' old adversaries, the Pharisees, were accusing Him of being in league with the devil. Because Jesus was casting out devils, He was accused of getting help from Beelzebub, the prince of the devils. Jesus stated that if He were truly the help of Satan, it would be a case of Satan destroying his own kingdom.

how are the mighty fallen!

The beauty of Israel is slain upon thy high places: **how are the mighty fallen***!* (2 Samuel 1:19)

In this day and age of sports heroes and entertainment icons, we are always seeing some of the famous lose all integrity because of scandal or behavior. The phrase "how are the mighty fallen" is used to describe their fall. These religious superstars, entertainment icons, and sports heroes are merely human. Only God Almighty rules and reigns forever.

I

if need be

*Wherein ye greatly rejoice, though now for a season, **if need be,** ye are in heaviness through manifold temptations.* (1 Peter 1:6)

Peter spoke of the saints' faith being tried "if need be" through many temptations. This simple phrase unlocks the mystery of why believers are tempted and tried. In the plan of an unsearchably wise God and loving father, trials are deemed necessary. There is a purpose to trials, even if no one but God understands the reason behind them.

in all his glory

*And why take ye thought for raiment? Consider the lilies of the field, how they grow; they toil not, neither do they spin: And yet I say unto you, That even Solomon **in all his glory** was not arrayed like one of these.* (Matthew 6:28–29)

To be "in all your glory" signifies that you are showing off peculiar attributes, good or bad, that truly exemplify yourself to others. It can also mean you are stark naked! When the multitudes were worried about things like food and clothing, Jesus told them a flower was grander than the richest king's splendor. God sure knew how to put things in perspective, wouldn't you say?

in God's hands

*FOR all this I considered in my heart even to declare all this, that the righteous, and the wise, and their works, are **in the hand of God**: no man knoweth either love or hatred by all that is before them.* (Ecclesiastes 9:1)

I remember watching the 1994 NBA Finals between the Houston Rockets and the New York Knicks and seeing the expression "In God's hands" written, of all places, on the head of one of New York's players. He obviously thought the outcome of the game depended on God's will. The meaning of this biblical phrase signifies both the inability of man to control their lives and God's "hands on" care for any situation. As master craftsmen of many sorts use their hands to mold and shape their creation, so does God Almighty mold and shape His own.

in God we trust

In God have I put my trust: *I will not be afraid what man can do unto me.* (Psalm 56:11)

What person is on every coin and paper bill in America? Well, it's not "Old George" or "Honest Abe," but God Himself, except He didn't get His picture on them, just His name inside the familiar phrase, "in God we trust."

We are, of course, not to put our trust in man, as the context of the phrase "in God we trust" indicates. As Christians, we are not even supposed to put our trust in other Christians. God certainly doesn't, as stated in Job 15:15: "Behold, he putteth no trust in his saints: yea, the heavens are not clean in his sight." God can't count on any man, but man can definitely count on God.

in the blink (twinkling) of an eye

In a moment, **in the twinkling of an eye,** *at the last trump: for the trumpet shall sound, and the dead shall be raised incorruptible, and we shall be changed.* (1 Corinthians 15:52)

Better known as "in the blink of an eye," this expression is used to denote things happening in an instant, like the actual blink of an eye. In this passage, God talks of changing our bodies "in the twinkling of an eye" at the rapture of the saints.

in the heat of battle

*And he wrote in the letter, saying, Set ye Uriah **in** the forefront of **the hottest battle**, and retire ye from him, that he may be smitten, and die.* (2 Samuel 11:15)

Sporting events, particularly football and hockey, often give rise to confrontations that are the result of the intense competition or the "heat of the battle." King David's actions exemplified the meaning of this expression when he ordered Uriah to go to the front lines of battle. He did this hoping to get Uriah killed so he could have Uriah's wife Bathsheba for himself.

in the spirit

*I was **in the Spirit** on the Lord's day, and heard behind me a great voice, as of a trumpet.* (Revelation 1:10)

The apostle John was literally "in the spirit" when he was caught up to heaven and shown visions of God and the future. To do something "in the spirit" of someone or something means that one is agreeable and enthusiastic about something or is in harmony with it. The phrase as it used today has nothing to do with God.

in your right mind

*And they come to Jesus and see him that was possessed with the devil, and had the legion, sitting, and clothed, and **in his right mind**: and they were afraid.* (Mark 5:15)

Jesus, and even Paul, cured demon-possessed people instantly and completely, so completely, in fact, that afterwards, one was said to be "in his right mind," or completely normal. This wasn't your ordinary demon possession, for this man that Jesus cured had broken chains that were put on him and was seen mutilating himself and hanging around tombs.

it is high time

And that, knowing the time, that now <u>**it is high time**</u> *to awake out of sleep: for now is our salvation nearer than we believed.* (Romans 13:11)

This phrase continues to be used of events or actions that seem on the brink of being late. Believers often live in just this manner, ignorant of the brief amount of time left to awaken from the sleep of apathy and act on faith.

J

jot and tittle

For verily I say unto you, Till heaven and earth pass, one **jot or one tittle** *shall in no wise pass from the law, till all be fulfilled.* (Matthew 5:18)

Those who work with contracts or detailed paperwork can appreciate the phrase "jot and tittle." It is equivalent to "dotting your '*i*'s' and crossing your '*t*'s,' or paying close attention to details. If we want to know God's attitude toward His Word, this quotation by Jesus should provide us with that.

To show the importance of a single letter, the apostle Paul based a whole doctrine on the letter "*s*," the difference between "*seed*" and "*seeds*." In Galatians 3:16, he makes his case: "Now to Abraham and his seed were the promises made. He saith *not*, And to *seeds*, as of many; *but* as of one, And to thy *seed*, which is Christ."

The next time you're in a biblical discussion and someone says you're arguing over semantics, tell this person that semantics are exactly what you should be debating. Ask any lawyer how much semantics matter, and he'll explain that it is not only the words that matter, but also the letters themselves.

Judgment Day

Verily I say unto you, It shall be more tolerable for the land of Sodom and Gomorrha in **the day of judgment,** *than for that city.* (Matthew 10:15)

This phrase speaks of impending crisis where action or an explanation is due. In the biblical sense, everyone will "get their day in court." The judge will be Jesus Christ, and the true Judgment Day will begin. The defendant will have no lawyer. There will be no trial by jury. There will be no adjudicated probation or shortened sentences for good behavior. The death penalty awaits those who have rejected Jesus as their advocate and Savior.

The possibility of a complete pardon does exist, but it must be obtained from Jesus Himself before the trial begins. No law degree is needed for that, but a knowledge of His law is essential.

jump for joy

Rejoice ye in that day, and **leap for joy**: *for, behold, your reward is great in heaven: for in the like manner did their fathers unto the prophets.* (Luke 6:23)

We usually use "jump for joy" when we feel extreme happiness or elation. Some people say they are "on cloud nine" while others are "walking on air."

Jesus told us to actually "jump," and He said to do it for a reason we wouldn't expect. In verse 22 of the above reference, He had this to say: "Blessed are ye, when men shall hate you, and when they shall separate you from their company, and shall reproach you, and cast out your name as evil, for the Son of man's sake. Rejoice ye in that day, and leap for joy."

Christians must realize they will, at times, be hated. Jesus said if people hated Him, they will hate us also. Rejoice and leap for joy!

just say the word

The centurion answered and said, Lord, I am not worthy that thou shouldest come under my roof: but **speak the word only,** *and my servant shall be healed.* (Matthew 8:8)

The expression, "Just say the word" is often used by a person who is ready and willing to do whatever another desires.

The centurion and the Christian have a lot in common. Both recognize the need for authority and obedience to it. In another sense, both are soldiers who should be prepared for war at anytime.

keep the faith

I have fought a good fight, I have finished my course, I have **kept the faith***:* (2 Timothy 4:7)

Not wavering, waffling, or turning back on what we believe qualifies as "keeping the faith." The world has a similar saying: "If you don't stand for something, you'll fall for anything." Paul refused to compromise his beliefs and was ready to receive his crown in heaven. Notice it says "the faith," which implies that there is only one faith.

Compromise in matters of faith and other areas of our life is praised today as a noble quality to possess. For a Christian to compromise would be the "kiss of death" (see **kiss of death** on p. 195).

The world says compromise shows evidence of our tolerance. God, on the other hand, wants us to stand up for our principles and never compromise our convictions or tolerate sin.

kill the fatted calf

And he said unto him, Thy brother is come; and thy father hath **killed the fatted calf***, because he hath received him safe and sound.* (Luke 15:27)

Another way of saying, "Let's have a dinner party" is to tell everyone you're going to "kill the fatted calf." This expression originates from the parable of the prodigal son told by Jesus. After his wayward son returned home, the father welcomed him with open arms, an obvious parallel to God opening His arms to the wayward sinner.

kingdom come

Thy **kingdom come**. *Thy will be done in earth, as it is in heaven.*
(Matthew 6:10)

The more popular meaning of "kingdom come" is to die; it also means something will take so long a time in coming that it probably won't occur. Examples would be: "a nuclear bomb would blow us all to kingdom come" or "You can keep arguing till kingdom come, but I won't change my mind."

Taken from the Lord's Prayer, "kingdom come" alludes to the coming of the kingdom of God.

know-it-all

Hast thou perceived the breadth of the earth? declare if thou **knowest it all**. (Job 38:18)

The only real know-it-all (because He does literally know everything) is God, Himself. Anyone else that is called that name acts as if he has all knowledge, something akin to what Job did when God asked him some rather tough questions.

God was showing the finiteness of Job in comparison to Himself. It is when we admit that we don't know it all that God chooses to work with us.

L

labor of love

Remembering without ceasing your work of faith, and **labor of love,** *and patience of hope in our Lord Jesus Christ, in the sight of God and our Father.* (1 Thessalonians 1:3)

A hobby or job that one does for the sheer pleasure that he or she gets from it can be called a "labor of love." Paul commended the church at Thessalonica for their work for the Lord. For any true Christian, doing the Lord's work is an honor and is naturally a labor of love. If you don't like doing the work of God such as witnessing, teaching, and helping others, but you do it anyway, your labor is in vain and is more like a "labor of necessity." If anyone loves working for his or her boss, it should definitely be the Christian.

land of giants

And the rest of Gilead, and all Bashan, being the kingdom of Og, gave I unto the half tribe of Ma-nasseh; all the region of Argob, with all Bashan, which was called the **land of giants.** (Deuteronomy 3:13)

Some of you might be old enough to remember the old television show called *Land of the Giants,* where the little people were always hiding from the giants. The Bible mentions giants, so naturally such biblical accounts of vertically-blessed people are ridiculed and scoffed at by skeptics as being false. What the Bible referred to as "giants" were men that were probably nine to ten feet tall.

There is archaeological evidence for these men, and we've even had modern examples of men that grew to almost nine feet tall (see the *Guinness Book of World Records*). The Israelites mentioned seeing giants in the land of Canaan and said they were the sons of Anak. Of course, we all know the story of Goliath, the giant of Gath, and how David killed him with a slingshot.

land of milk and honey

And I am come down to deliver them out of the hand of the Egyptians, and to bring them up out of that land unto a good land and a large, unto a **land flowing with milk and honey***; unto the place of the Canaanites, and the Hittites, and the Amorites, and the Perizzites, and the Hivites, and the Jebusites.* (Exodus 3:8)

Sounds like an enormous candy bar or some recipe for a sore throat, but this expression was a description of the fertile lands of Israel. Today, even as in the days of Moses, a "land of milk and honey" describes any fertile land ripe for settlement.

God promised the land of the Canaan to the Hebrew slaves. This is the root of the controversy in the Middle East today.

land of the living

But where shall wisdom be found? and where is the place of understanding? Man knoweth not the price thereof; neither is it found in **the land of the living***.* (Job 28:12–13)

The "real world" is a saying with the same meaning as the colorful expression "land of the living." It is often used to welcome back people who have stayed out of the public eye for some reason. This meaning hasn't changed much from the biblical usage where Job mentioned that wisdom wasn't found in the "land of the living."

The apostle Paul adds to this teaching when he said, "The wisdom of this world is foolishness with God." Try posting that on some college billboard. Real wisdom comes from God, not necessarily from the college professor who teaches in the "land of the living."

laugh to scorn

All they that see me **laugh me to scorn***: they shoot out the lip, they shake the head, saying. . . .* (Psalm 22:7)

This passage in the Psalms prophesies of Jesus' suffering on the cross and His famous "Why hast thou forsaken me" quote. Jesus' enemies actually laughed at Him while He hung on the cross. They didn't just laugh, but "laughed to scorn," or to the point of vehement ridicule.

Ah, but let us not forget who gets the last laugh (see **he who laughs last** on p. 194). In Psalm 2:4, God said He (the Father) will actually laugh and hold in derision those who try to plot against Him. When God laughs, it's not funny.

laughter is the best medicine

A merry heart doeth good like a medicine*: but a broken spirit drieth the bones.* (Proverbs 17:22)

Scientists say that laughter actually helps by producing chemicals in our bodies that relieve stress and benefit us physically and mentally. The Bible essentially says the same thing, only a few thousand years before it was actually scientifically proven.

Yet there seems to be a conflict. The Bible says, "A merry heart doeth good like a medicine," but it also says "Sorrow is better than laughter." Crying is better than laughing? Yes, ". . . for by the sadness of the countenance the heart is made better" (Ecclesiastes 7:3).

We could all use a good laugh, but what we really need even more is a good cry.

law unto themselves

*For when the Gentiles, which have not the law, do by nature the things contained in the law, these, having not the law, are **a law unto themselves**.* (Romans 2:14)

Disobeying established authority and setting ourself up as our own judge makes us "a law unto ourself." As with many of these expressions, the Bible's use of it is literal, not figurative. Paul spoke of the Gentiles' own conscience serving as the law that would judge them because of their lack of a written law at that time.

God, then, agrees with the adage, "Let your conscience be your guide," because God's laws are "written in their hearts" (v. 15). Only to the extent that one doesn't have a Bible and can't get one should conscience be the guide.

There is a point, however, that the wicked reach when even their consciences can't guide them anymore because they have become "seared with a hot iron" (1 Timothy 4:2). The best remedy— let the Bible be your guide.

lay at the door of . . .

*If thou doest well, shalt thou not be accepted? and if thou doest not well, sin **lieth at the door**. And unto thee shall be his desire, and thou shalt rule over him.* (Genesis 4:7)

When we say something is "lying at the door," usually we signify that something bad is about to happen. God stated that sin was lying at the door of Cain if Cain didn't do well. God also said that sin would "rule" over Cain and that "sin" would be Cain's desire.

Sadly, this is the case for every sinner. Sin rules over everyone who has not experienced victory over it through Christ. Paul stated in Romans 6:6–7 that sin doesn't rule over the Christian: "Knowing this, that our old man is crucified with *him*, that the body of sin might be destroyed, that henceforth we should not serve sin. For he that is dead is freed from sin." In Romans 6:14, he teaches that ". . . sin shall not have dominion over you: for ye are not under the law, but under grace."

If sin is lying at your door, you can bet it will get its foot in. Sin is the biggest and most powerful "Pandora's box."

lay down your own neck

Who have for my life **laid down their own necks***: unto whom not only I give thanks, but also all the churches of the Gentiles.* (Romans 16:4)

To sacrifice yourself for another is the current as well as the biblical meaning for "laying down your own neck." The apostle Paul expressed his affection for his friends Aquila and Priscilla who he said "laid down their own necks" for him. The measure of true love, according to Jesus, is found in John 15:13: "Greater love hath no man than this, that a man lay down his life for his friends."

The fact that God actually laid down His own life on the cross provides us with the single greatest act of love ever shown. God did not send someone else to die for us; He Himself became a man by being born of a virgin. In 1 John 3:16, the Bible states very clearly: "Hereby perceive we the love of God, because he laid down his life for us: and we ought to lay down *our* lives for the brethren." What greater sacrifice and act of love could God have shown us?

left hand doesn't know what the right hand is doing

But when thou doest alms, let not thy **left hand know what thy right hand doeth***.* (Matthew 6:3)

The phrase "left hand doesn't know what the right hand is doing" speaks of a group of people working together but pulling in different directions because they're unorganized or are being given conflicting orders. In other words, they're not all on the same page. How's that for defining an expression with another expression! One sure way people can truly be on the same page is for them to get their marching orders from the Bible.

lesser light

And God made two great lights; the greater light to rule the day, and the **lesser light** *to rule the night: he made the stars also.* (Genesis 1:16)

The "lesser light" referred to here is probably the moon, and the greater light is likely the sun. Notice how nonchalantly the Bible mentions "he made the stars also." Over one hundred billion stars, each being thousands of times bigger than the earth, were made—and God made them all.

The expression "lesser light" currently refers to someone who is not as well-known as others but is still respected. That meaning is carried over into the biblical realm as well. We are all "lesser lights" compared to Jesus, "the light of the world."

The sun and the moon being called the greater and the lesser lights is a perfect illustration of the relationship of Jesus to the believer. The sun generates its own light and causes the moon to shine, just as Jesus the Son gives the moon (the believers) His light, and we shine it upon the world (the earth). The moon has no light or life of its own, and it even has a dark side (which represents the believer's old nature). Though the moon only reflects the sun's light, it is the brightest light in the darkness of night.

An eclipse of the moon happens when the moon gets between the sun and the earth. When that happens in analogy, the moon (the believer) stops shining because it is blocking the sun's light from reaching earth, just like the Christian (the moon) can get in the way of the world seeing Jesus the Son (sun). What beautiful object lessons God has given us!

let come what may

Hold your peace, let me alone, that I may speak, and **let come on me what will.** (Job 13:13)

"Let the chips fall where they may," "Whatever happens, happens,"—these are similar in meaning to the biblical expression that Job used when he told his detractors that no matter what happened to him, he would say to God, ". . . let come on me what will." Job's faith and trust in God is legendary and is exemplified in his statement two verses later: "Though he slay me, yet will I trust in him: but I will maintain mine own ways before him."

The world might have to rely on chips falling where they may or supposed good luck, but the Christian shouldn't believe in or rely on luck. The Scriptures don't wish us "good luck" but say in Romans 8:28: "And we know that all things work together for good to them that love God, to them who are the called according to his purpose."

let nature take its course

And the tongue is a fire, a world of iniquity: so is the tongue among our members, that it defileth the whole body, and setteth on fire the **course of nature;** *and it is set on fire of hell.* (James 3:6)

The Bible says in the next two verses that humans have tamed every type of animal, yet the tongue remains untamed and can't be tamed, for "it is an unruly evil, full of deadly poison." To "let nature take its course" implies that nature operates in a systematic way, or by course, and that it will take care of itself as long as man's tongue doesn't set it on fire.

Nature doesn't have a mind of its own, but only operates and takes its course because of what God has programmed it to do. How else would animals have the instincts they do if it were not for those instincts having been put into the animals in the first place?

God tells us that we can tame animals, yet we struggle to tame the tongue.

like father, like son (like mother, like daughter)

Behold, every one that useth proverbs shall use this proverb against thee, saying, **As is the mother, so is her daughter.** *(Ezekiel 16:44)*

Parents can attest to the truthfulness of this adage because they know their children will, in part, reflect their own values. Children are the fruit of their parents, and a "tree is known by its fruit." The same idea holds true in the spiritual sense as well. Jesus told the Pharisees in John chapter eight: "Ye are of *your* father the devil, and the lusts of your father ye will do."

We are either children of God or children of the devil according to the Bible; there is no in-between state or neutrality with God. The prevailing notion that all people are God's children is obviously false.

like putty in my hand

O house of Israel, cannot I do with you as this potter? saith the Lord. Behold, **as the clay is in the potter's hand,** *so are ye in mine hand, O house of Israel. (Jeremiah 18:6)*

Being called "putty in my hand" is considered a derogatory comment because the person that is labeled "putty" is thought to be easily manipulated by others. The Christian, however, considers it an honor to be putty in God's hands, for the clay, or putty, does not tell the potter how to shape it according to Romans 9:20: "Nay but, O man, who art thou that repliest against God? Shall the thing formed say to him that formed *it*, Why hast thou made me thus?"

The picture of the spinning clay pot being formed on the potter's wheel is the analogy that God wants us to imagine because He is rounding all our rough edges and shaping us into a beautiful vessel. God even calls us "vessels" in 1 Thessalonians 4:4. Vessels are used to pour liquid into, and God pours His spirit into each vessel He creates. We could all use a few lessons in the potter's class.

little bird told me

Curse not the king, no not in thy thought; and curse not the rich in thy bedchamber: for <u>a bird of the air shall carry the voice,</u> and that which hath wings shall tell the matter. (Ecclesiastes 10:20)

Surprisingly, this expression finds its origin from the book of Ecclesiastes. We use it today when we want to hide the source of particular information. In the context of this phrase, the Bible warns us not to curse others because a "bird of the air" might spread the word.

little by little

<u>By little and little</u> *I will drive them out from before thee, until thou be increased, and inherit the land.* (Exodus 23:30)

God told Israel He would drive out their enemies "by little and little." This idea has application in the spiritual sense in that God drives out our enemies, or sin, little by little so that we can learn the power of sin and the power of God to defeat it.

God, if He wanted, could give all of us lives without sin or death to deal with. But we should thank God for sin and death, for without it, many of us would not need, depend on, or seek

God. Death, though tragic, is also a tool that God uses to bring us closer to Him.

Because we are to thank God in everything ("In every thing give thanks"), we should not hesitate to thank Him for sin and death instead of always questioning why someone has to suffer or die.

live by the sword, die by the sword

Then said Jesus unto him, Put up again thy sword into his place: for all <u>they that take the sword shall perish with the sword.</u> (Matthew 26:52)

A very appropriate philosophy of modern-day street gangs, this saying originated from the mouth of Jesus at the time of His arrest and betrayal by Judas. Peter pulled out his sword and cut off the ear of one of the high priest's servants during the arrest of Jesus. Jesus rebuked Peter for cutting the servant's ear off and actually put it back on without plastic surgery!

live for one's self

And that he died for all, that they which live should not henceforth <u>live unto themselves,</u> *but unto him which died for them, and rose again.* (2 Corinthians 5:15)

Everybody lives for something, whether it's money, fame, work, family, etc. If there comes a time when these don't matter anymore, we say we have "nothing to live for."

The whole Christian walk is the process of not "living for one's self," but living for the God who died for them. Telling someone to "get a life" is what the Christian has actually done, for he or she are recipients of "the way, the truth, and the life."

live off the fat of the land

*And take your father and your households, and come unto me: and I will give you the good of the land of Egypt, and ye shall eat **the fat of the land**.* (Genesis 45:18)

To "live off the fat of the land" is to live in luxury or to enjoy the best a place has to offer. Pharaoh told the Israelite Joseph, his second-in-command, that Joseph and his family had that privilege in Pharaoh's country.

We in America have been living off "the fat of the land" for years, but it's possible that all of this luxurious living could come to a screeching halt. America needs to turn its eyes back to the Lord or face sure judgment.

lord and master

*Ye call me Master and Lord; and ye say well; for so I am. If I then, your **Lord and Master**, have washed your feet; ye also ought to wash one another's feet.* (John 13:13)

This expression is often a sarcastic euphemism for one's husband and if used in the literal sense would be scoffed at today. If a man states that he is "lord and master" of the house, he will probably receive a good laugh. Yet, in the truest sense, God has made the man the head of a household.

If the wife recognizes that the man is the "master of the house," she wouldn't have any problem obeying him. Men are called the masters of the house several times in Scripture (see Judges 19:23), but women are never referred to this way. We obey our bosses because they have the final authority at our jobs, so why do some have problems with God placing the final authority in the home with the husband? After all, you can't have two masters at home or the job.

Lord have mercy

Have mercy upon us, O **LORD, have mercy** *upon us: for we are exceedingly filled with contempt.* (Psalm 123:3)

Commonly used as an exclamation of help or astonishment, this biblical expression has literal meaning for King David who wanted God's mercy granted unto him continually. Pleading for mercy occurs often in courtrooms. Sometimes mercy is granted. God, the judge of all, always grants mercy to those who sincerely ask for it.

"Lord have mercy" has been so overused that many of us may not realize it is a plea for God to shed His mercy on us because of our sins. If you don't have it, don't leave this earth without it, or "Lord have mercy!"

lost and found

For this my son was dead, and is alive again; he was **lost, and is found**. *And they began to be merry.* (Luke 15:24)

We normally look for lost valuables in the "lost and found" department of some establishment, but on the bigger scale, God looks in the heavenly "lost and found," for to Him, the whole human race could be classified as "lost and found" in His eyes because they're either saved (found) or lost (damned).

A "lost and found" scenario occurs in the story of the prodigal son. Here, a wayward son was lost but was later found. "Lost" is the right description for the person without God. Just like the lost traveler, the wayward sinner rarely admits that he is lost. God provides a spiritual road map and waits at the door with open arms for all those wanting to come home.

M

make a name for yourself

And they said, Go to, let us build us a city and a tower, whose top may reach unto heaven; and let us **make us a name***, lest we be scattered abroad upon the face of the whole earth.* (Genesis 11:4)

Trying to get recognition and prestige for yourself defines this expression from the book of Genesis. The builders of the ill-fated Tower of Babel tried to "make a name for themselves," and God showed them how He felt about this by destroying the tower and making all humankind speak different languages.

The existence of languages like Chinese, Russian, German and others with all their vast differences and complete lack of connection to each other goes to show that this judgment at Babel not only could have happened, but actually did happen.

make a spectacle of yourself

For I think that God hath set forth us the apostles last, as it were appointed to death: for **we are made a spectacle** *unto the world, and to angels, and to men.* (1 Corinthians 4:9)

Drawing attention to yourself in a foolish way is considered "making a spectacle of yourself." Paul said that the apostles are "made a spectacle unto the world" and, in like manner, so are all Christians. If you are a believer, you will be ridiculed for believing in talking snakes (the garden of Eden), Noah's ark, nine hundred-year-old men (Genesis 5), people making the sun stand still (Joshua), and so on. Believers are accounted as "fools for Christ's sake" because of their witness, actions, and beliefs.

make bricks without straw

Ye shall **no more** give the people **straw to make brick**, as heretofore: let them go and gather straw for themselves. (Exodus 5:7)

"Making bricks without straw" is the perfect motto for the employee who is given a job to do but not the resources to do it. "Making bricks without straw" is what Pharaoh commanded the Israelites to do after Moses asked Pharaoh to let him and the Hebrews go to the desert to offer sacrifices and worship to their God. Pharaoh's response to the taskmasters was to make the slaves' work harder by ordering them to make bricks without straw. The addition of straw, of course, made it easier to make bricks. The upshot of the whole affair was that Pharaoh believed that the Hebrews' religion was getting in the way of their work.

make light of

*But they **made light of** it, and went their ways, one to his farm, another to his merchandise.* (Matthew 22:5)

In the parable of the marriage of the king's son, the invited guests made light of their invitations and went their own ways in much the same way that some make light of being invited to the marriage supper of the lamb, Jesus Christ.

make your hair stand on end

*Then a spirit passed before my face; **the hair of my flesh stood up**.* (Job 4:15)

Job's friend, Eliphaz, reminded Job in this passage that suffering came because of sin. Eliphaz recounted how a "spirit" (He didn't say it was God) appeared and spoke to him, giving Eliphaz wisdom. (How many times do we hear that today?) Job was not impressed with his friend's wisdom or visions, and we too should be skeptical when others say they have received a vision from the Lord. Eliphaz said, "The hair of my flesh stood up"; in other words, he was terrified.

God's spirit shouldn't terrify believers. So what Eliphaz saw was undoubtedly not a manifestation from God. The Christian world today has many people seeing so-called "visions" and hearing many voices. If you want to hear God's voice, then read His Word. You won't have to wonder whose voice you're hearing.

man after your own heart

But now thy kingdom shall not continue: the LORD hath sought him <u>a man after his own heart</u>, and the LORD hath commanded him to be captain over his people, because thou hast not kept that which the LORD commanded thee. (1 Samuel 13:14)

A person "after your own heart" shares your beliefs and values, akin to a soul mate. When King Saul reigned over Israel, the prophet Samuel told the king that because of Saul's disobedience, God sought "a man after His own heart" to be the next king of Israel. That man turned out to be David. In like manner, anyone who has "kept that which the Lord commanded" can also be a man (or a woman) after God's own heart.

man child

And when the dragon saw that he was cast unto the earth, he persecuted the woman which brought forth the <u>man child</u>. (Revelation 12:13)

An immature adult or extremely large baby could be called a "man child." The Bible's use of "man child" is quite the opposite, for it designates Jesus Christ as the "man child" in the book of Revelation.

Jesus must have acted like a man even when He was a little child because He confounded the scholars in the Temple at the age of twelve with His biblical wisdom. It is always sad to see Christian children today who confound unlearned adults with their wisdom.

man of the house

*And wheresoever he shall go in, say ye to the good***man of the house***, The Master saith, Where is the guestchamber, where I shall eat the passover with my disciples?* (Mark 14:14)

The expression, "man of the house," usually refers to the father of a family, but with today's staggering divorce rate, is becoming less and less applicable. In too many homes today, there is no man of the house, and in a lot of homes where a man or "father-figure" does exist this person doesn't act like a father-figure.

Jesus spoke of a certain house where He wanted His disciples to eat the Passover supper and called the owner the "goodman of the house." Jesus implied that this man was the head of the house just as the Bible does in other passages where it calls the man the "master of the house." The Bible specifically calls the husband "the head of the wife" in Ephesians 5:23, and in Genesis 3:16, God told Eve that her "desire *shall be* to thy husband, and he shall rule over thee."

Some people fault the Bible for making gender distinctions. The Bible indeed states that there are certain roles for a wife and certain ones for a husband. However, we should realize that a husband and a wife are equals in God's sight, but that God specifically tells a wife to willingly place herself, as an equal, up under her husband's leadership because this is God's design. When a Christian wife follows God's design, she shows evidence of the Holy Spirit in her life.

man of the world

Arise, O Lord, disappoint him, cast him down: deliver my soul from the wicked, which is thy sword: From men which are thy hand, O

Lord, from **men of the world**, *which have their portion in this life, and whose belly thou fillest with thy hid treasure: they are full of children, and leave the rest of their substance to their babes.* (Psalm 17:14)

Though used to describe cultured, sophisticated men, "men of the world" are the ones David asked God to deliver him from. A Christian should never consider it a compliment to be called a "man of the world." How we feel about worldly people, possessions, and events is a surefire test of how we feel about God. "If any man love the world, the love of the Father is not in him."

manna from heaven

And had rained down **manna** *upon them to eat, and had given them of the corn* **of heaven**. (Psalm 78:24)

What we all would like during our time of need is some manna from heaven, an unexpected, timely, even miraculous gift like the Israelites received in the desert when they had no food to eat. Their "manna" was a type of bread that literally came down from the skies to feed them during their Exodus through the desert.

many a time

Many a time *have they afflicted me from my youth: yet they have not prevailed against me.* (Psalm 129:2)

A quaint way of saying that you have experienced something rather frequently is by using the expression "many a time." This saying is found in Psalms, where King David speaks of the afflictions he received from the wicked occurring "many a time."

Life is no bed of roses for a Christian, for "Many *are* the afflictions of the righteous: but the LORD delivereth him out of them all" (Psalm 34:19).

meat and drink to someone

For the kingdom of God is not **meat and drink***; but righteousness, and peace, and joy in the Holy Ghost.* (Romans 14:17)

Anything important, essential, or pleasing to you could also be designated as your "meat and drink." Exercise is meat and drink to an athlete as book reading is to a scholar. The modern usage of this phrase differs from its biblical counterpart. In Romans, Paul teaches that "meat and drink" (i.e., dietary concerns) are not concerns of those in the kingdom of heaven.

What a concern food is, however, for those on earth! Think of the time we spend buying, preparing, eating, and cooking food, and don't forget about the dishes! Eating consumes a substantial part of the average person's life.

Will we eat food in heaven? Who knows? Jesus ate broiled fish and honeycomb after He came back from the dead and from paradise (see Luke 24:42), so it stands to reason that Christians after death can do the same. However, we won't need this food to keep us alive since we will be perfected in body and soul.

Pizza, ice cream, and fried chicken may not be on the menu. Our diets will might even consist of what Adam and Eve had in the garden, but we won't have to worry about any forbidden fruit. We will be eating from the Bread of Life of whom it is said, "he that cometh to me shall never hunger; and he that believeth on me shall never thirst."

meet your maker

Therefore thus will I do unto thee, O Israel: and because I will do this unto thee, prepare to **meet thy God***, O Israel.* (Amos 4:12)

We will all "meet our Maker" one day, as we will be face-to-face with the Creator of the universe, Jesus Christ. God told a backsliding Israel that because of their sins, He was getting ready to destroy them and told them they should "prepare to meet thy God."

It's sad that most of the time when we hear this phrase, it's in the context of someone who is not ready to "meet their Maker" and are being told to get ready to meet Him because of his or her impending death. We all should prepare a little better for that meeting. We might want to take a few notes ahead of time because that's a meeting we can't miss.

millstone (albatross) around your neck

But whoso shall offend one of these little ones which believe in me, it were better for him that a **millstone were hanged about his neck,** *and that he were drowned in the depth of the sea.* (Matthew 18:6)

A heavy burden of responsibility one has to bear is also called an "albatross around the neck" or "millstone" as the Scripture calls it. The context of this phrase has Jesus speaking of children and giving a warning that it is a grave offense for adults to corrupt these children and their beliefs. Jesus said these evil corrupters would be better off if they had "drowned in the depths of the sea" because the punishment that awaits them is much worse than they can imagine.

Jesus was not saying all children are innocent, for there comes a time when each child must exercise faith and trust in Him. Exactly when that time arrives varies with each child, but it corresponds with the time when they can understand that they are sinners and that Jesus paid the price for their sins with His death and His blood.

mind your own business

And that ye study to be quiet, and to **do your own business,** *and to work with your own hands, as we commanded you.* (1 Thessalonians 4:11)

"Keeping your nose out of other people's affairs" is the meaning of this biblical expression from Paul's letter to the Thessalonians. Scripture admonishes believers in another passage not to be "busy bodies," but, instead, "with quietness they work, and eat their own bread" (2 Thessalonians 3:12).

Working is a commandment of God, and those who refuse to work aren't supposed to get charity or even food given to them: "For even when we were with you, this we commanded you, that if any would not work, neither should he eat" (2 Thessalonians 3:10).

morning, noon, and night

Evening, and morning, and at noon, *will I pray, and cry aloud: and he shall hear my voice.* (Psalms 55:17)

"Morning, noon, and night," as used in this Scripture, is not a prescription for the exact times you should pray as the Muslims have adopted, but it is an admonition to pray at all times as it states in 1 Thessalonians 5:17: "Pray without ceasing." This expression is used today to emphasize something that happens constantly; thus, it retains the biblical meaning as well. Notice, however, that the Bible says evening comes first, for the biblical day starts with the night and ends with the daylight.

mother of all . . .

And Adam called his wife's name Eve; because she was **the mother of all** *living.* (Genesis 3:20)

The Persian Gulf War made this expression popular again when Saddam Hussein said that the approaching war would be "the mother of all battles" meaning the greatest and grandest of all. The Bible used this phrase in the literal sense, referring to Eve as the actual "mother of all living."

If you like tracing your family tree, you might not be able to totally complete it, but you will know who your oldest relatives are because everyone came from the same parents, Adam and Eve. The "mother of all" of us was Eve. A question that regularly comes up is how Adam and Eve could have accounted for all the different races in the world. It is possible that God made Adam and Eve's sons and daughters different ethnicities, for Adam had all the genes of future man in his body. In reality, this is a question that will never be fully answered this side of heaven.

my cup runneth over

Thou preparest a table before me in the presence of mine enemies: thou annointest my head with oil; **my cup runneth over**. (Psalm 23:5)

Akin to the picture of the "horn of plenty," the phrase, "my cup runneth over," is another vivid illustration of the bountifulness of God's blessings for His children. In the famous twenty-third psalm, David mentioned walking through the infamous "valley of the shadow of death" at the same time that he said his "cup runneth over."

This is the comfort Christians can have in the midst of strife: God can make your cup run over even when you are facing death itself. As a Christian, you will always have plenty because you will always have God, who Paul said in Philippians 4:19, "shall supply all your need according to His riches in glory by Christ Jesus."

N

next of kin

None of you shall approach to any that is **near of kin** *to him, to un-cover their nakedness: I am the* LORD. (Leviticus 18:6)

Frequently, we hear this expression used when someone dies or is killed. The name of the deceased often isn't released until the next of kin is notified, that is, the closest relatives of the deceased. "Kin" is a country dialect, and the Bible contains other examples of country talk.

The Bible is truly a book for all people, appealing to the scholar, the common man, and the unlearned through its use of differing styles of language. It's even a little bit "country."

nothing new under the sun

The thing that hath been, it is that which shall be; and that which is done is that which shall be done: and there is **no new thing under the sun**. (Ecclesiastes 1:9)

Go into any supermarket and you'll see products advertising something "new," "advanced," or "improved." Science and technology continually bombard us with the newest research and inventions. According to God, none of this is new whatsoever. We are always discovering things about ancient civilizations that show they had advanced ideas in science or math that we previously thought we had invented.

Even the Bible alludes to numerous scientific facts that were supposedly only "discovered" in this modern era. For example, the fact that the earth is a sphere and not flat (as was believed in the Middle Ages) could easily have been discredited with a reading of Isaiah 40:22: "It is he that sitteth on the circle of the earth."

The Bible has always been way ahead of its time and is much more scientifically correct than it usually gets credit for.

now hear this

Therefore **now hear this**, *thou that art given to pleasures, that dwellest carelessly, that sayest in thine heart, I am, and none else beside me; I shall not sit as a widow, neither shall I know the loss of children.* (Isaiah 47:8)

Commonly used as an attention-getting gimmick over a megaphone or microphone, this adage was employed by God to warn Babylon of its coming judgments. It was a serious warning then, but now it is usually relegated to a practical joke, as when someone is trying to act as if an important announcement is going to be made.

God won't need a public address system to announce His coming to the earth. "For the Lord himself shall descend from heaven with a shout," it says in 1 Thessalonians 4:16. Instead of the "*shot* heard 'round the world," God will have His "*shout* heard 'round the world."

O

oh my God!

O my God, my soul is cast down within me: therefore will I remember thee from the land of Jordan, and of the Hermonites, from the hill Mizar. (Psalms 42:6)

A plea for help and a cry to God has been turned into a trite saying that is used so much now that it has lost its original force and is now used just the same as an ordinary exclamation like "Wow" or "Gee." Even heathen, atheists, and agnostics occasionally exclaim "Oh my God" despite the fact they don't really believe in Him.

Isn't it ironic that unbelievers call on God even when they profess to hate Him? There is no escaping the influence of the Bible on lives of the ordinary citizen because God will make sure you learn of Him whether you want to or not.

oh spare me!

O spare me, that I may recover strength, before I go hence, and be no more. (Psalms 39:13)

"Spare me, please" is the cry of those who do not want to hear something or who disapprove of a matter rather strongly. David asked God to literally spare him, or preserve his life; thus, the meaning has changed again from literal to figurative though there is a slight connection still to the biblical usage.

old days

The Lord hath done that which he had devised; he hath fulfilled his word that he had commanded in **the days of old***: he hath thrown down, and hath not pitied: and he hath caused thine enemy to rejoice over thee, he hath set up the horn of thine adversaries.* (Lamentations 2:17)

The old days often bring back fond memories for those of us who can remember the way things used to be. With things changing so fast these days, there are fewer things to remind us of the way life was many years ago.

The Bible is certainly a living link with the old days, because parts of it have been around for thirty-five hundred years. God's Word is the one item that many families have shared over scores of generations. The fact that our lives are being shaped today by the same book that our ancestors had thousands of years ago is astounding, and it is a testament to the enduring value of this amazing book. The "old days" will always be here to some degree as long as we have the Bible.

old wives' tales

But refuse profane and **old wives' fables***, and exercise thyself rather unto godliness.* (1 Timothy 4:7)

The term "old wives' tales" is used as a description for superstitions and folk tales that have been passed down over the years. The expression probably refers to a time when most women were uneducated and their words lacked credibility. The fables spoken of in 1 Timothy 4:7 belonged to the category of silly superstitions. In other words, we should pay no attention to outlandish myths.

once and for all

*By the which will we are sanctified through the offering of the body of Jesus Christ **once for all**.* (Hebrews 10:10)

Christians are sanctified (saved) "through the offering of the body of Jesus Christ once *for all*." The blood of Jesus paid for all of our sins—past, present, and future. Anything added to that sacrifice would make a mockery of the greatest act of love ever shown to humankind.

Too many churches and religious systems lead their members to believe that you get to heaven by believing and earning your way there. Therefore, many people are under the impression that they must go to church, give money, ask for forgiveness, be baptized, do good deeds, speak in tongues, and so forth, or else they won't get to heaven. Many of these confused souls will tell you that Jesus is "the Way," even though their actions and attitudes reveal that they think they are "the way to the Way."

one and the same

*But all these worketh that **one and the selfsame** Spirit, dividing to every man severally as he will.* (1 Corinthians 12:11)

Writing about the spiritual gifts to the church, Paul was making the point that though there were diversities of operations and administrations of God, it was all done by the "same spirit" (verse 4), the "same Lord" (verse 5), and the "same God" (verse 6).

Since humans were created in God's image and likeness, all of us bear a resemblance to Him. Therefore, we all have one soul, one body, and one spirit just as God does in the person of Jesus Christ. Jesus and God are "one and the same."

one way or another

*Go thee **one way or other**, either on the right hand, or on the left, whithersoever thy face is set.* (Ezekiel 21:16)

God told the prophet Ezekiel to either go "one way or other," to the right or to the left, and God would cease His judgments on Israel. The expression "one way or another" refers to the desire to get something done no matter what it takes.

If we analyzed this phrase more closely, we would recognize that it conveys further biblical truth. There is only "one way" or "the other"—God's way or Satan's. There is the "broad way" or the "narrow way" according to Matthew 7.

out of sight, out of mind

*I am forgotten as a dead man **out of mind**: I am like a broken vessel.* (Psalms 31:12)

"How soon we forget" goes the old saying. When someone we have shared company with no longer sees us, or when we ignore a matter for a time, we tend to forget about that person or thing because he, she, or it is "out of sight, out of mind." David was lamenting over the fact that no one seemed to be mindful of his plight, so he said he felt like a "dead man out of mind."

Fortunately God doesn't do the same to those who keep Him out of sight and out of mind, for if He did, none of us would ever be blessed of God. "The LORD hath been mindful of us: he will bless *us*" (Psalm 115:12). We will never be out of sight and out of mind with God.

out-of-the-body experience

*I knew a man in Christ above fourteen years ago, (whether in the body, I cannot tell; or whether **out of the body**, I cannot tell: God knoweth;) such an one caught up to the third heaven.* (2 Corinthians 12:2)

Paul recounted how he knew a man who was "caught up to the third heaven" and heard things he said were "not lawful for a man to utter." Some believe Paul was referring to himself in the third person, speaking of the time perhaps when he was stoned and left for dead.

Regardless of who is being talked about, we hear this type of thing occurring regularly. For example, some people claim to have died clinically, gone to heaven, saw lights, and felt total peace. Did you ever notice that none of these people ever seem to die and get a vision of hell?—it's always heaven. Out-of-the-body experiences, however, are nothing new, and everyone will participate in one at the time of their death—some just get a little preview, like Paul.

out of the mouth of babes

<u>Out of the mouth of babes</u> *and sucklings hast thou ordained strength because of thine enemies, that thou mightest still the enemy and the avenger.* (Psalms 8:2)

Little children have a way of stating the simple truths that adults often overlook. The simple, yet blunt truth, will often come from a child and can teach us many things. On the other hand, to use this expression to teach that little children always speak the truth is wrong. According to Psalm 58:3: "The wicked are estranged from the womb: they go astray <u>as soon as they be born, speaking lies</u>."

How do infants speak lies, you ask? Become a parent and you'll find out. Little babies are capable of deceiving without us even realizing it. They learn to cry for things even when they're not upset, and this is not learned but bred in them.

P

parting of the ways

For the king of Babylon stood at the **parting of the way**, *at the head of the two ways, to use divination: he made his arrows bright, he consulted with images, he looked in the liver.* (Ezekiel 21:21)

After several unsuccessful attempts to reach an agreement on a matter, individuals might have what is called "a parting of the ways." The apostle Paul, to much surprise, had one of these "parting of the ways" arguments with one of his associates. Barnabas wanted to take John Mark along with Paul to visit several churches that Paul had established. Paul was adamant about not taking John Mark as Acts 15:38–39 states: "But Paul thought not good to take him with them, who departed from them from Pamphylia, and went not with them to the work. And the contention was so sharp between them, that they departed asunder one from the other; and so Barnabas took Mark, and sailed unto Cyprus."

In the context of Ezekiel where another "parting of the ways" occurs, the king of Babylon, after coming to a fork in the road, was confused about which way to go, so he tried various methods, including witchcraft and looking at livers. How a liver can tell one which direction to take has to qualify as one of the stranger ways to get one's bearings, but, then again, when people don't have God to lead them, they might try anything.

pass the time

And if ye call on the Father, who without respect of persons judgeth according to every man's work, **pass the time** *of your sojourning here in fear:* (1 Peter 1:17)

When there's nothing to do, and you're looking for something to help occupy your time, God says to "pass your time" or live your life in reverent fear. In Proverbs 23:17, the Bible says to "Let not thine heart envy sinners: but *be thou* in the fear of the LORD all the day long."

Instead of killing time, the Christian's obligation is to make the most of every opportunity, "because the days are evil" (Ephesians 5:16).

passed away

One generation **passeth away**, and *another* generation cometh: but the earth abideth for ever. (Ecclesiastes 1:4)

To blatantly say a friend or loved one has died can be a little difficult for some, so saying this person "passed away" softens the blow a little. Death is part of living—we can't escape death. So whether we die or "pass away," the Christian has the hope and promise of a new life, and there is joy in that assurance.

patience of Job

Behold, we count them happy which endure. Ye have heard of **the patience of Job***, and have seen the end of the Lord; that the Lord is very pitiful, and of tender mercy.* (James 5:1)

James, the brother of Jesus, instructed Christians to be patient concerning the coming of the Lord, for many saints were growing restless for Christ's return. To understand and appreciate the expression "patience of Job," you need to be familiar with the account of Job and his sufferings.

As it turned out, Job lost everything—his family, his health, his fortune, and his friends. Throughout his ordeal, and despite occasional weakness, Job believed in the goodness of God. In the end, God gave double to him back of what he had lost.

Though the patience of Job is quite commendable, the patience of God is exceedingly more so.

patience of a saint

Here is **the patience of the saints***: here are they that keep the commandments of God, and the faith of Jesus.* (Revelation 14:12)

We are called to endure many trials in this life. For some, those troubles lead to untold anxieties. To curse God and die would be the easy way out. But for those who face the distresses and misfortunes of life with a positive outlook, they are labeled as having the "patience of a saint."

It needs to be pointed out that those who follow God are called "saints" in the Scriptures (see Jude 14; Philippians 1:1; Deuteronomy 33:2, etc.). All believers are saints.

peace and quiet

And the work of righteousness shall be **peace; and** *the effect of righteousness* **quiet**ness *and assurance for ever.* (Isaiah 32:17)

The cry of every parent with unruly children is for a little "peace and quiet." The need for peace and quiet is a universal need. The Bible says that the righteousness that comes from God brings peace, and the effect of righteousness will produce quietness. A wicked person can never truly have peace and quiet even if he surrounds himself with life's pleasures, for "There is no peace, saith my God, to the wicked" (Isaiah 57:21).

pearl of great price

Again, the kingdom of heaven is like unto a merchant man, seeking goodly pearls: Who, when he had found one **pearl of great price***, went and sold all that he had, and bought it.* (Matthew 13:45–46)

The "pearl of great price" is an object that is so important to us that we willingly give up everything to own it. In this parable of Jesus, the man who saw the pearl did not speculate for there was no risk in buying the pearl. He knew its intrinsic value. Opportunity had presented itself. As a result of his discovery, the man gives up all he has to gain the one thing he desires.

Some people, even in their forties, give up a reputable job and enter seminary to pursue the pastorate. Others may leave an established medical practice to become missionaries in the far corners of the world. And for others like Chuck Colson or Deion Sanders, it maybe giving up fame and fortune to follow Christ

To discover the "pearl of great price" is to discover the will of God for your life. And whether this discovery is a sudden illumination or the discovery at the end of a long search—the pearl is worth everything.

Without hesitation or question, do accept it!

pearly gates

And the twelve **gates were twelve pearls***; every several gate was of one pearl: and the street of the city was pure gold, as it were transparent glass.* (Revelation 21:21)

The commonly quoted misconception that Peter stands at "the pearly gates" checking our names on the list is not biblically accurate. Actually, twelve angels will stand at twelve different gates of pearl, not Peter. Many people don't realize that these pearly gates are part of the superstructure of the gigantic city called "New Jerusalem." This city is described as being in the shape of a cube, fifteen hundred miles ("fifteen thousand furlongs") long, wide, and high. The whole city is surrounded by a wall that is over three hundred feet high (144 cubits).

Citizenship requirements are strict, yet simple: You must be a Christian. Inside the city are the famous "streets of gold"; in fact, everything in it is made of pure gold. The city will actually descend from heaven and be placed on earth by God Himself at His return. New Jerusalem will be the most magnificent sight you will ever see outside of seeing Jesus Christ.

play the fool

*Then said Saul, I have sinned: return, my son David: for I will no more do thee harm, because my soul was precious in thine eyes this day: behold, I have **played the fool**, and have erred exceedingly.* (1 Samuel 26:21)

"Everybody plays the fool, sometimes. There's no exception to the rule." Remember these words from the old pop song? King Saul of Israel said he "played the fool" after he had been pursuing David in an effort to kill him. At the same time, however, Saul was being threatened by his enemies, which gave David a chance to kill King Saul. David refused to do so, and this action convicted Saul so much so that he admitted that he "erred and played the fool" in trying to kill David.

Foolishness in Scripture is always associated with wickedness: "The foolishness of man perverteth his way: and his heart fretteth against the LORD." According to Jesus, the wisest man to ever live even tried foolishness: "I applied mine heart to know, and to search, and to seek out wisdom, and the reason *of things*, and to know the wickedness of folly, even of foolishness *and* madness" (Ecclesiastes 7:25). Man likes to think foolishness is cute, but God thinks differently.

powers that be

*Let every soul be subject unto the higher powers. For there is no power but of God: **the powers that be** are ordained of God.* (Romans 13:1)

We hear this often in reference to our bosses at work or anyone who is in charge. "The powers that be" has particular relevance to governmental leaders that the Bible says are "ordained of God" no matter who they are.

That means God places people in positions of power—from Julius Caesar to Adolf Hitler to George W. Bush—for His own reasons, whether it is to punish a nation and cause it to repent or bless a nation for its faithfulness. God will ordain whomever He wants regardless of campaign promises or political maneuvering. Thus, Jesus can't be labeled a Republican, Democrat, Independent, Fascist, or Socialist because He has ordained rulers from all these persuasions at one time or another.

pride goes before a fall

Pride goeth before destruction, *and an haughty spirit before a fall.* (Proverbs 16:18)

We can often trace someone's downfall to a person's pride, according to the Bible. Actually, the verse quoted says that pride leads to destruction and also a fall. The fall of man in the Garden of Eden involved Adam's pride. It was Adam's pride that led him to eat the fruit: "For all that *is* in the world, the lust of the flesh, and the lust of the eyes, and the pride of life, is not of the Father, but is of the world" (1 John 2:16).

People will usually blame their own downfall on circumstances beyond their control, but rare is the occasion when a person points to his or her own pride as the reason. We are told to take pride in our accomplishments. However, the Bible tells us that "God resisteth the proud, but giveth grace unto the humble" (James 4:6). If we want to take pride in things, we must be prepared for a "double whammy"—our own downfall and resistance by God.

promised land

By faith he sojourned in the **land of promise***, as in a strange country, dwelling in tabernacles with Isaac and Jacob, the heirs with him of the same promise.* (Hebrews 11:9)

If we want to know the cause of the Middle East peace problem, we need look no further than the promise of land (promised land) that God made to Abraham in Genesis 15:18: "In the same day the LORD made a covenant with Abram, saying, Unto thy seed have I given this land, from the river of Egypt unto the great river, the river Euphrates."

The problem stems from the fact that Abraham's firstborn son, Ishmael, through his maid Hagar, while Isaac came through his wife Sarah. As was the custom, the firstborn son was to inherit most of his father's property. God, however, recognized Isaac as the only legitimate heir. Thus, the descendants of Isaac, the Jews, and the descendants of Ishmael, the Arabs, fight to this very day over who owns the birthright to Abraham's promised land.

The Arab contention that Ishmael's descendants should be the heir is clearly refuted in such passages as Genesis 21:12: "And God said unto Abraham, Let it not be grievous in thy sight because of the lad, and because of thy bondwoman; in all that Sarah hath said unto thee, hearken unto her voice; for in Isaac shall thy seed be called."

prophet without honor

And they were offended in him. But Jesus said unto them, **A prophet is not without honour***, save in his own country, and in his own house.* (Matthew 13:57)

A prophet without honor is one that doesn't get the recognition he deserves, especially from his own country or town. Jesus said all of Israel's prophets received dishonor and even death at the hands of their own countryme. The same fate would not pass by Jesus Christ who was the ultimate prophet without honor.

pull out of the fire

*And others save with fear, **pulling them out of the fire**; hating even the garment spotted by the flesh.* (Jude 23)

Rescuing someone from a hostile or dangerous situation could also be called "pulling out of the fire." As used in the Word of God, "pulling out of the fire," means delivering an individual from the impending sentence of hell by helping that person accept salvation through Christ. Even though this individual is not in the fiery torment, God implies that the person is so close that he should be dragged away from it.

Christians take on many roles, and helping sinners by pulling them out of the fire makes the Christian a true fire fighter.

put it on my tab

*If he hath wronged thee, or oweth thee ought, **put that on mine account**.* (Philemon 18)

"Put it on my tab," we like to say. Although there were no charge cards in Paul's day, he was willing to have charged to his account any wrongdoings his friend Onesimus might have committed. This action demonstrated the heart of the gospel: the innocent willing to suffer for the guilty.

Most of us have a hard enough time suffering for our own guilt much less the guilt of others. The debt that each of us owes for sin is one tab that can't be paid by us. The fact that Jesus took on the sin of the world at the Cross showed that He paid the biggest one-time bill ever accumulated—for we all put it on His "tab," and He willingly paid it.

put words in someone's mouth

And come to the king, and speak on this manner unto him. So Joab <ins>put the words in her mouth</ins>. (2 Samuel 14:30)

When we tell someone what we think he or she is trying to say, that individual will often fire back and say, "Don't put words into my mouth." In biblical usage, Joab, an Israelite army captain, is said to have "put words into the mouth" of a woman named Tekoah. Joab wanted to use this woman to deceive King David by telling her the words to say to the king.

Putting words into people's mouths is precisely what God did to all the prophets who uttered or wrote His words as recorded in the Bible: "As for me, this *is* my covenant with them, saith the LORD; My spirit that *is* upon thee, and my words which I have put in thy mouth, shall not depart out of thy mouth, nor out of the mouth of thy seed, nor out of the mouth of thy seed's seed, saith the LORD, from henceforth and for ever" (Isaiah 59:21).

put your hand to the plow

And Jesus said unto him, No man, having <ins>put his hand to the plough</ins>, and looking back, is fit for the kingdom of God. (Luke 9:62)

This is another of Jesus' so-called "hard sayings." Some misinterpret this quote to mean that if we as believers go astray, we are "not fit." Jesus teaches in this verse that if we are double-minded and unsure of whether or not we want to follow Him, we are unfit.

"Putting your hand to the plow" means you are preparing to work hard to give it your all. There should be no hesitance in a person in making a decision for kingdom work, but if there is, that person is not yet ready or fit for God's kingdom.

Q

quick and the dead

I charge thee therefore before God, and the Lord Jesus Christ, who shall judge **the quick and the dead** *at his appearing and his kingdom.* (2 Timothy 4:1)

Though a popular title for books and movies (see Appendix D), "the quick and the dead" signifies the living and the dead whom Jesus will judge at His Second Coming. Though He's judging the quick, it's not the swift He's talking about, but the living.

Whether a criminal is living or dead affects the likelihood that he can get out of paying for his crime. We can't bring a dead man to justice, but Jesus can and will. One day, He will raise all the dead and judge them, and then cast many of the same into eternal judgment.

R

race is not to the swift

I returned, and saw under the sun, that <u>the race is not to the swift,</u> *nor the battle to the strong, neither yet bread to the wise, nor yet riches to men of understanding, nor yet favor to men of skill; but time and chance happeneth to them all.* (Ecclesiastes 9:11)

Remember the fable of the tortoise and the hare? That theme is the meaning of the biblical saying "the race is not to the swift." The winner is not always the fastest, smartest, or strongest, but he is the one who is the wisest and most persistent. It is ironic that this was the finding of King Solomon, who was the smartest and strongest king who ever lived.

Notice that we are indeed in a "race," not a rat race as the world would have us believe, but a race that is to be run with patience according to Hebrews 12:1. The Christian's race makes all who run in it a winner, for the prize is eternal life with Jesus Christ.

The apostle Paul used the very same language when he wrote to the church at Philippi: "I press toward the mark for *the prize* of the high calling of God in Christ Jesus" (Philippians 3:14; see **eyes on the prize** on p. 191). It's not who has the most toys that wins, but who has the right prize.

reap what you sow

Be not deceived; God is not mocked: for <u>whatsoever a man soweth, that shall he also reap</u>. (Galatians 6:7)

"What goes around comes around" and "You'll get what's coming to you" are equivalent expressions that have to do with a person getting what he deserves for some unseemly action he has committed. The Bible acknowledges the laws of nature. Just as the farmer gets what he plants, the same is true in the spiritual world. The right soil, the right fertilizer, and plenty of water will produce a good crop as well as a good Christian. You can't fool Mother Nature, and you definitely can't fool Father God.

return to the fold

And I will gather the remnant of my flock out of all countries whither I have driven them, and **will bring them again to their folds;** *and they shall be fruitful and increase.* (Jeremiah 23:3)

Used to denote a person returning to a group he once belonged to, the phrase "return to the fold" in the biblical context refers to Israel returning to its homeland after being driven to other countries. God blamed the pastors for driving them away as it is recorded in the previous verse in Jeremiah 23:2: "Therefore thus saith the Lord God of Israel against the pastors that feed my people; Ye have scattered my flock, and driven them away...."

God says in verse 4 that He would "set up shepherds over them which shall feed them." Obviously then, the shepherds and pastors were not feeding the people of Israel.'

If you have wandered away from the church and the Lord, you need to "return to the fold."

right in your own eyes

The way of a fool is **right in his own eyes:** *but he that hearkeneth unto counsel is wise.* (Proverbs 12:15)

One characteristic of a fool is that he thinks he's always right. Since he's only right in his own eyes, he accepts no other arguments. If we are right in our own eyes, then we don't consider other viewpoints.

Christians are often labeled as "arrogant" and "right in their own eyes." This expression is directed toward Christians who are unwavering in their commitment to God. Those who criticize devout Christians think that right and wrong is not measured by how much black and white you see in issues, but in how much gray you perceive. Christians who believe in absolutes are construed as narrow minded and unobjective.

The argument, however, is not whether the Christian is right or wrong; it is whether the Bible is right or wrong. God is the only One who is truly right in His own eyes; to question God's objective truth will make you wrong in His eyes.

ripe old age

And Gideon the son of Joash died in **a good old age***, and was buried in the sepulchre of Joash his father, in Ophrah of the Abi-ezrites.* (Judges 8:32)

"Only the good die young" goes the popular saying. To live long, or to a "ripe old age," is not limited to only those who do wrong, but it is also attainable for those who do good. One of the Ten Commandments promises that children will live long if they obey their parents: "Honor thy father and thy mother: that thy days may be long upon the land which the LORD thy God giveth thee" (Exodus 20:12).

rise and fall of . . .

And Simeon blessed them, and said unto Mary his mother, Behold, this child is set for **the fall and rising again of** *many in Israel; and for a sign which shall be spoken against. . . .* (Luke 2:34)

This saying is reversed in modern usage and finds its place in the titles of many books and movies. David Bowie entitled one of his best-selling albums *The Rise and Fall of Ziggy Stardust and the Spiders from Mars*. Many famous achievers are known for rising to the top and then falling out of the limelight.

God speaks of Israel falling first and then rising again in the last days to a prominence she had never before attained. Rising and falling is exactly what happened to the nation of Israel. It fell to the Romans in A.D. 70 and was completely annihilated to the point of losing its national borders and ceasing to exist as a country. Almost nineteen hundred years later in 1948, Israel, through the providence of God, became a nation again—despite the surrounding nations' attempt to thwart it. God is now readying the world for the rising again of Israel to fulfill His plan for the end times.

rise and shine

<u>Arise, shine</u> *for thy light is come, and the glory of the LORD is risen upon thee.* (Isaiah 60:1)

Used regularly as the morning trumpet song in the army, "rise and shine" is the universal language for "get up and get out of bed." The Bible says we are to "rise and shine" because God's Light has come in the person of Jesus Christ.

One can tell the difference between a child of God and a child of the devil by the shine that God puts on his or her face. In Philippians 2:15, God says, "That ye may be blameless and harmless, the sons of God, without rebuke, in the midst of a crooked and perverse nation, among whom ye shine as lights in the world."

Jesus is "the light of the world"; only the Son makes us truly shine.

root of all evil

For the love of money is **the root of all evil***: which while some coveted after, they have erred from the faith, and pierced themselves through with many sorrows.* (1 Timothy 6:10)

Often, this expression is misquoted as saying, "Money is the root of all evil." This rendering changes the entire meaning of the verse. It is "the *love* of money" that is the "root of all evil." To find out the causes of most examples of corruption, "follow the money trail" as some would say.

rooted and grounded in . . .

That Christ may dwell in your hearts by faith; that ye, being **rooted and grounded in** *love, may be able to comprehend with all saints what is the breadth, and length, and depth, and height.* (Ephesians 3:17–18)

When you know something backwards and forwards and know it like the back of your hand, you were probably rooted and grounded in it by much study or experience. Being rooted and grounded in genuine love and pure doctrine is the foundation for a strong and growing Christian life.

root (heart) of the matter

But ye should say, Why persecute we him, seeing **the root of the matter** is found in me? (Job 19:28)

Trying to get to the bottom of something is akin to finding out "the root of the matter." As used in the Scriptures, the phrase "the root of the matter" is employed by Job when his so-called friends blamed Job for his own suffering. Job said that "the root of the matter" or the cause of his emotional suffering was his so-called friends. Job denied their accusation, and rightly so, for God Himself acknowledged Job as a "perfect" or righteous man (see Job 1:1).

Job was a fine example of the phrase "with friends like these, who needs enemies." These people who pretended to be Job's friends were nothing more than wolves in sheep's clothing (see **wolves in sheep's clothing**) who manipulated the word of God just enough to cause confusion. Job saw through it and did not fall for their false praise and false condemnation cloaked in the guise of religion. The Bible is an excellent tool for helping you get to "the root of the matter."

ruin of someone

For he sacrificed unto the gods of Damascus, which smote him: and he said, Because the gods of the kings of Syria help them, therefore will I sacrifice to them, that they may help me. But they **were the ruin of him***, and of all Israel.* (2 Chronicles 28:23)

King Ahaz thought that if the gods of the kings of Syria helped the Syrians, they should work for him also, so he worshiped them.

Doesn't this sound all too familiar? Some say, "Why don't we take what works for the world and put it to use in the church? Since it has been successful for some, we can make it successful for us; only, let's modify it somewhat and make it look more church-like." A good rule of thumb to remember: If the world thinks highly of something, God probably doesn't, because "that which is highly esteemed among men is abomination in the sight of God" (Luke 16:15).

rule with an iron hand

And out of his mouth goeth a sharp sword, that with it he should smite the nations: and he shall **rule them with a rod of iron***: and he treadeth the winepress of the fierceness and wrath of Almighty God.* (Revelation 19:15)

Most often, this expression applies to a harsh, strict boss or political leader who severely punishes disobedience. This same meaning turns up in the Book of Revelation in regard to the reign of Jesus Christ who it says will also rule with an iron hand or "rod of iron."

Naturally, Jesus will have the power no other leader has ever had to crush any opposition to His rule, and He won't need a military to do it. "Every knee shall bow" to the King of kings in fear or in worship. Jesus will rule with an iron hand over those who oppose Him.

run for your lives

And it came to pass, when they had brought them forth abroad, that he said, <u>**Escape for thy life**</u>*; look not behind thee, neither stay thou in all the plain; escape to the mountain, lest thou be consumed.* (Genesis 19:17)

The destruction of Sodom and Gomorrah for their iniquity was delayed mercifully by God until God's angels took Lot and his family out. Lot was told to "escape for thy life" or, as we say today, "run for your life." According to Scripture, God brought a reluctant Lot from out of the wickedness of Sodom. God always knows what is better for us.

S

safe and sound

And he said unto him, Thy brother is come; and thy father hath killed the fatted calf, because he hath received him **safe and sound**. (Luke 15:27)

From the story of the prodigal son comes the cliché, "safe and sound." The reference is to the wayward son who returned home "safe and sound" after realizing the error of his ways.

This parable provides us with other common expressions such as "lost and found," "kill the fatted calf," and "riotous living." One reason for this story's popularity is that it parallels the lives of many parents who have children that rebel. The parents prayer is that their children will recognize that the prodigal way of living is an endless street of brokenness, despair, and spiritual hunger.

Jesus, like the father in the parable, will not stop those who want to pursue prodigal living, but He will always be waiting for those who realize they need Him.

salt of the earth

Ye are **the salt of the earth**: *but if the salt have lost his savor, wherewith shall it be salted? it is thenceforth good for nothing, but to be cast out, and to be trodden under foot of men.* (Matthew 5:13)

You can't give a finer compliment to another than to describe a person as "the salt of the earth," which simply means that person is the best or noblest of people. Christians, according to Jesus, are the "salt of the earth," preserving, as salt does, the virtues of God and applying them to a world that is decaying. Because Jesus distinguished Christians as the "salt of the earth," it is biblically incorrect to call anyone else the same title.

saving grace

Even when we were dead in sins, hath quickened us together with Christ, (by **grace ye are saved***).* (Ephesians 2:5)

A "saving grace" as it is used today speaks of a particular quality of a person or thing that keeps he, she, or it from being all bad. Grace, in the biblical sense, is undeserved or unmerited favor. In other words, God provides or gives us what we don't deserve.

The word "save" has become so adulterated with all the world wanting to "save the whales," "save the trees," "save the ozone layer," and "save money" that the concept of saving one's soul doesn't have the impact it used to. Yet only through the saving grace of God can a person be eternally saved. No efforts of man can duplicate the salvation God provides to those who trust in Him.

scales (blinders) fell from your eyes

And immediately there **fell from his eyes as it had been scales:** *and he received sight forthwith, and arose, and was baptized.* (Acts 9:18)

After Paul literally saw the light (see **see the light**) of Jesus on his way to Damascus, he was temporarily blinded for three days. A disciple named Ananias was instructed by God to lay hands on Paul. He did so, and Paul received his sight back as the "scales" fell from his eyes. "Blinders on the eyes" is the modern equivalent, but it means the same—something that is keeping you from seeing the whole picture.

Jesus describes all those outside the kingdom of God as "blind." Everyone that is spiritually blind needs God to remove the blinders from their eyes.

scum of the earth (filth of the world)

Being defamed, we intreat: we are made as **the filth of the world,** *and are the offscouring of all things unto this day.* (1 Corinthians 4:13)

"Scum of the earth" is the ultimate insult. Many in today's media view evangelical Christians at the bottom of the totem pole—the "scum of the earth." In today's anti-Christian climate, Christians get little or no respect. Any Christian who wants to get respect from the world will need to put his Christianity on the backburner.

Jesus was viewed as the "scum of the earth" in His day, and the same is true of Christians in the twenty-first century.

see eye to eye

The watchmen shall lift up the voice; with the voice together shall they sing: for they shall **see eye to eye,** *when the LORD shall bring again Zion.* (Isaiah 52:8)

Agreeing with each other and sharing a common understanding could be deemed "seeing eye to eye." The Bible prophesied of a time when God's people would see eye to eye because Jesus would be reigning in Zion and everything would be right. This expression is usually used in the negative sense when it says people "don't see eye to eye."

People don't like to look each other in the eyes if they don't like one another. There's something about the eyes that reveal a person's heart; hence, the expression, "The eyes are the windows of the soul." Those that don't want you to see their eyes may be doing so in an effort to prevent you from seeing their soul.

seeing is believing

The other disciples therefore said unto him, We have seen the Lord. But he said unto them, __Except I shall see__ in his hands the print of the nails, and put my finger into the print of the nails, and thrust my hand into his side, __I will not believe.__ (John 20:25)

A skeptical world today demands proof of something by seeing it, for to them, "seeing is believing." To the Christian, seeing is not necessarily believing as Hebrews 11:1 states: "Now faith is the substance of things hoped for, the evidence of things *not seen.*" Jesus further stated that "blessed *are* they that have not seen, and *yet* have believed" (John 20:29).

The interesting thing about someone demanding to see so that he can believe is actually a belief proven wrong in many instances in Scripture. In Luke 16:30–31, the rich man who was in torment in hades told Abraham that he had five brothers that would repent "if one went unto them from the dead." The response by Abraham debunks the "seeing is believing" philosophy: "And he said unto them, If they hear not Moses and the prophets, neither will they be persuaded, though one rose from the dead."

Many people say if they could only see Jesus or witness miracles they would believe in Christianity. According to the Bible, if they saw these things, they still wouldn't believe. Many people saw Jesus work miracles, but not all believed. Belief requires faith, which is an act. It is not an automatic reaction to miracles seen. Faith in Jesus Christ is not merely acknowledging Him, but it is trusting and loving Him with all your heart.

seek and ye shall find

Ask, and it shall be given you; <u>seek, and ye shall find</u>*; knock, and it shall be opened unto you.* (Matthew 7:7)

A popular quotation as well as biblical expression, "seek and ye shall find" is used by Jesus in His Sermon on the Mount speech when He tells the multitudes to "ask," "seek," and "knock."

Seeking God is no different. People will often claim they have tried sought God or found the truth, but they end up frustrated. This sounds like a noble effort until you realize that God says you can only find Him when you seek Him with your *whole* heart and nothing less: "And ye shall seek me, and find *me*, when ye shall search for me with all your heart" (Jeremiah 29:13).

This is the true meaning of "seek, and ye shall find." It's really very simple: if you haven't found God, maybe you haven't searched for Him with your whole heart.

see the light

He will deliver his soul from going into the pit, and his life shall <u>see the light</u>. (Job 33:28)

Job's friend Elihu gave his prescription for attaining righteousness by saying that if any man says he has sinned, God will rescue him from the pit, and he will "see the light." To "see the light" is to fully grasp the meaning or importance of a matter. We often use this expression in a biblical sense to describe one who sees the light of Jesus, the Light of the world.

Some use this expression jokingly or derisively to mock those who have turned their lives over to the Lord.

see the light of day

Let the stars of the twilight thereof be dark; let it look for light, but have none; <u>neither let it see the dawning of the day</u>. (Job 3:9)

Telling someone that he won't "see the light of day" is a warning that he is about to be incarcerated or prevented from living a normal life, usually because of something that person did. It could also mean something won't come to fruition or come to pass; hence, it won't see the light of day that is coming.

Job was cursing the day he was born for all his suffering, and the Bible says he desired for the stars not to see the "dawning of the day." Job questioned why God gave him wisdom: *"Why is light given to a man whose way is hid, and whom God hath hedged in?"* (Job 3:23).

That is a good question. Why does God give wisdom to those people who are "hid" and "hedged" in? The reason is that God uses the foolish things of this world to confound the wise. He also is a God that hides His truth from the wicked: "Verily thou *art* a God that hidest thyself" (Isaiah 45:15).

see to it

When Pilate saw that he could prevail nothing, but that rather a tumult was made, he took water, and washed his hands before the multitude, saying, I am innocent of the blood of this just person: **see ye to it.** (Matthew 27:24)

Pilate didn't want to take responsibility for the fate of Jesus—especially after the uproar of the crowd—so he "washed his hands" of the matter (see **wash your hands of something**). He told the Jews to "see ye to it" and handle the matter themselves. The Jews saw to it and crucified Jesus, despite the fact that Pilate declared Him a "just person."

This incident exemplifies pure democracy in action which inevitably results in mob rule. Since democracy is the rule of the people, if the will of the majority is corrupt (and it is quite often), so will be the government. There are other examples of the democratic process in the Bible. Almost every time democracy is practiced in

Scripture, the people choose a corrupt leader or go against the will of God. Two prime examples of this are the choosing of Aaron as leader of the Israelites while God was giving Moses the Law (Exodus 32:1) and Saul as King of Israel (1 Samuel 8:5–6). Both of these actions led to the corruption of Israel.

God doesn't spiritually sanction a democracy any more than He does a dictatorship, though Americans strongly contend that our form of government is the godliest. We also like to think that the majority always knows what is right, yet scores of ungodly laws have been passed in this nation in the name of "majority rule."

separate the sheep from the goats

And before him shall be gathered all nations: and he shall **separate** *them one from another, as a shepherd divideth his* **sheep from the goats.** (Matthew 25:32)

To organize or put things or people into different groups is to "separate the sheep from the goats." When Jesus separates the sheep from the goats, He will distinguish between the believers and the unbelievers, the believers being the sheep, and the goats being the unbelievers.

Perhaps we often see goats cast in a negative light and sheep in a good light because of this parable told by Jesus.

sell one's soul

For what is a man profited, if he shall gain the whole world, and lose his own soul? or what shall a man give in **exchange for his soul**? (Matthew 16:26)

This passage has been made famous by the story of *Faustus,* a story of a doctor who sells his soul to the devil for worldly gain.

When someone sells his soul today, it speaks of selling out or giving in to whatever desires he has to the point of forsaking everything else.

Jesus asked His disciples and those who read this passage of Scripture to reflect on the value of the soul. If something is worth more to us than everlasting life, we can never receive God's gift. Nothing in the whole world should be more important to us than our souls.

sell your birthright

And Jacob said, Swear to me this day; and he sware unto him: and he sold his birthright *unto Jacob.* (Genesis 25:33)

If you "sell your birthright," you are usually giving up your claim for something valuable to someone else or exchanging it for something else. As was the custom back then and still today in some countries, the firstborn male child receives a significantly greater portion of the birthright or inheritance than does his siblings. Esau in this passage of Scripture was willing to sell his birthright for a "mess of pottage." Esau said he was so hungry he was "at the point to die," so Jacob took advantage and told him he would give him pottage or lentils if Esau would exchange his birthright for it. Esau agreed and Jacob got the birthright.

It is interesting that this passage does not mention that Jacob took advantage of his brother's hunger. Instead, the Bible points out that Esau "despised his birthright" by selling it to Jacob, thus teaching the importance of our inheritance as children of God.

Jesus Himself was the "firstborn from the dead," and we are heirs through Him according to Romans 8:17: "And if children, then heirs; heirs of God, and joint-heirs with Christ."

set your teeth on edge

In those days they shall say no more, The fathers have eaten a sour grape, and the children's teeth are set on edge. (Jeremiah 31:29)

Did you ever notice that our teeth really do line up on edge when we are nervous, anxious, mad, etc.? Of course, this reference in the Bible has the meaning of puckering up after eating something sour. Here, the Israelites were blaming an outside influence—their ancestors—for the bad situations in that nation. In Jeremiah's time, the Israelites claimed that their ancestors ate the sour grapes (see **sour grapes**), but that the current generation was actually receiving the sour, bitter, aftertaste. In other words, the Israelites of Jeremiah's time were tasting the dire consequences of the sins of many generations before them.

shake the dust off your feet (shake it off)

And whosoever shall not receive you, nor hear your words, when ye depart out of that house or city, **shake off the dust of your feet**. (Matthew 10:14)

Jesus' way of telling us not to get down when others won't receive our testimony of Him was to "shake off the dust of your feet." This saying is comparable to the expression "shake it off," which refers to someone ridding himself of some undesirable notion or feeling.

Sometimes Christians feel that if others aren't accepting their testimony, somehow, they did something wrong. Christians should expect most people to reject the truth.

shout it from the rooftops (housetops)

What I tell you in darkness, that speak ye in light: and what ye hear in the ear, that **preach ye upon the housetops**. (Matthew 10:27)

Getting excited about something and announcing it to the world at every opportunity is the meaning of this expression today.

Jesus told His disciples to preach the gospel, if need be, from the housetops.

There were no loudspeakers in the first century or megaphones to proclaim Jesus' message, so a housetop was one option. Today, we have numerous choices: housetops, megaphones, televisions, Internet, and so forth. The world today will not be happy if we unashamedly proclaim the gospel of Jesus, but Jesus expected us to proclaim His message as a normal course of action in the Christian life.

signs of the times

He answered and said unto them, When it is evening, ye say, It will be fair weather: for the sky is red. And in the morning, It will be foul weather to day: for the sky is red and lowring. O ye hypocrites, ye can discern the face of the sky; but can ye not discern **the signs of the times**? (Matthew 16:2–3)

Any characteristic that is indicative of modern-day society, especially if it's a negative one, is called a "sign of the times." Jesus said the Pharisees were able to read the sky and predict the weather, but they were unable to read the signs of the times. Jesus was pointing out the hypocrisy of keeping up with all the changing weather signs but ignoring the other signs that God gives a society on the brink of judgment.

Even the weather itself is a sign of the end times, as Jesus described the times just before His return by saying, "fearful sights, and great signs shall there be from heaven. . . . signs in the sun, and in the moon, and in the stars; and upon the earth distress of nations, with perplexity; the sea and the waves roaring" (Luke 21:21, 25). The expression, "How's the weather?" is a little more involved than you might think.

sing someone's praises

Then believed they his words; they **sang his praise**. (Psalms 106:12)

"Singing someone's praises" speaks of lauding and extolling a person greatly. If we need to sing someone's praises, let's do it for Someone who truly deserves it—Jesus.

sink into your ears

Let these sayings **sink down into your ears***: for the Son of man shall be delivered into the hands of men.* (Luke 9:44)

One of the many fitting expressions Jesus used was this one when He spoke to His disciples concerning His death. He didn't want there to be any misunderstanding of what He was saying, so He told them to let His sayings "sink down into your ears."

Although Jesus emphasized His death, they still didn't realize what He was talking about. It just didn't get into their "thick skulls" as we would say. Yet, as hardheaded as we are, God's words can still penetrate even the thickest of skulls.

sins of the fathers

And he walked in all **the sins of his father,** *which he had done before him: and his heart was not perfect with the* LORD *his God, as the heart of David his father.* (1 Kings 15:3)

The evil deeds of our ancestors are known as the "sins of the fathers." Though parents are responsible for the way they raise their children, kids are responsible for their own actions as well. While it is not inevitable that one generation will duplicate the sins of a previous one, history is replete with examples of corrupt leaders following their father's footsteps. For example, in 1 Kings, Abijam reigns in wickedness as did his father Rehoboam.

Throughout the media, we hear of parents being blamed for all the problems children are having. While it is perfectly true that parents sometimes influence their children negatively, this notion that kids aren't responsible for their actions because of the way they were raised is absurd. Even though there are sincere cases of child abuse and so forth, "the sins of the father" do not excuse any sins of the child.

sit in judgment on

A king that <u>sitteth in</u> *the throne of* <u>judgment</u> *scattereth away all evil with his eyes.* (Proverbs 20:8)

If there's one Scripture everybody knows, it's the one that says "judge not." If there were ever a verse that was yanked out of context, it is this one. The minute we sit in judgment on a matter, society will attack us and try to justify our attack biblically by quoting this "judge not" phrase from Matthew's Gospel.

Knowledgeable Christians won't fall for this stratagem, because Christians are commanded to judge all things: "But he that is spiritual judgeth all things, yet he himself is judged of no man" (1 Corinthians 2:15). If we are not to judge, then we couldn't distinguish between right and wrong.

When the Scriptures say, "Judge not, that ye be not judged," you never hear that second half of the verse that says, "For with what judgment ye judge, ye shall be judged"; thus, it is taken out of context. The Bible is not telling us to avoid judging, only that if we do judge others, we will be judged according to the same standard. That is a far cry from "Don't judge."

Think about this: When the world tells us that we shouldn't judge, they themselves are judging our commandment to judge.

sitting on top of the world

It is he that <u>sitteth upon the circle of the earth</u>, *and the inhabitants thereof are as grasshoppers; that stretcheth out the heavens as a curtain, and spreadeth them out as a tent to dwell in.* (Isaiah 40:22)

When we've got it made and are deemed successful, this qualifies us as "sitting on top of the world." Not surprisingly, this Scripture text applies literally to God of whom the Bible says that it is He only who "sitteth upon the circle of the earth" (Isaiah 40:22).

small beginnings

Though thy **beginning was small,** *yet thy latter end should greatly increase.* (Job 8:7)

Bildad the Shuhite spoke this verse to Job and predicted that the outcome of Job's suffering would be that his prosperity would "greatly increase." It actually did, because Job received twice as much after his suffering as he had before he had lost just about everything he owned. The common saying "small beginnings" speaks of something being insignificant at first but turning out to be very prolific later on.

Many Christians could testify how this expression is indicative of the way God operates in their lives. Insignificant, small events are the way God teaches us and causes things to happen in our lives. Later, we realize how these seemingly small beginnings turn out to be the catalyst for greater things down the road. God is in the small things as well as the big. When we begin to recognize His hand in everything, it is then that we truly begin to find satisfaction and joy in the Christian life.

so be it

And she said, According unto your words, **so be it.** *And she sent them away, and they departed: and she bound the scarlet line in the window.* (Joshua 2:21)

After Rahab hid the spies in her house and lied about it to their pursuers, she made a covenant with the spies and was promised protection by them in the upcoming battle. The Epistle to the Hebrews said Rahab received them by faith. Some commentators wonder how her lying was considered faith. It wasn't. She received the spies through faith, not through her lying. So be it.

sour grapes

What mean ye, that ye use this proverb concerning the land of Israel, saying, The fathers have eaten <u>sour grapes</u>, and the children's teeth are set on edge? (Ezekiel 18:2)

We all know the puckery sensation of eating a sour grape. Metaphorically, this is akin to the feeling of those in Ezekiel's and Jeremiah's time. But in this case, the forefathers ate the "sour grapes" or sowed the seeds of destruction while the descendants received the bitter aftertaste (see **set your teeth on edge**).

The Bible mentions that this expression was a proverb at the time of Ezekiel (594 B.C.), so this was an established proverb long before it showed up in Aesop's Fables from where many claim the phrase originated.

spare the rod, (spoil the child)

He that <u>spareth his rod</u> hateth his son: but he that loveth him chasteneth him betimes. (Proverbs 13:24)

In this day and age of lax discipline, parents would do well to take heed to this admonition. "Spoiling the child" was not part of the original quote, but it was added to make a truthful proverb. If we spare the rod according to the Bible, that means we hate our children. Wow! What a 180-degree turn from modern-day child rearing methods that verse is!

Child advocates constantly harp on how spanking is bad for children. Scripture refutes that notion and adds that neglecting to do so shows we don't care enough about our children. God never prescribed beating our children up, yet today, we have gotten far too lazy and complacent in our efforts to raise our children.

speak for yourself

Then Agrippa said unto Paul, Thou art permitted to **speak for thyself.** *Then Paul stretched forth the hand, and answered for himself.* (Acts 26:1)

Paul was on trial for his life, testifying before the king concerning his witness of Jesus. Paul was allowed to speak on his own behalf, but the expression "speak for yourself" has since come to mean, "Don't talk in the place of others or for others without their consent."

spirit is willing, but the flesh is weak

Watch and pray, that ye enter not into temptation: **the spirit indeed is willing, but the flesh is weak.** (Matthew 26:41)

Jesus recognized the two natures of mankind and how they war against one another. Paul also talked about the internal war that a Christian fights in Romans 7:23 when he states, "But I see another law in my members, warring against the law of my mind, and bringing me into captivity to the law of sin which is in my members."

No matter how strong and willing a Christian is, he or she has to admit the flesh is weak. Such an admission actually helps us get closer to Jesus, for when we are weak, He is strong.

spy out the land

These are the names of the men which Moses sent to **spy out the land.** *And Moses called Oshea the son of Nun Jehoshua.* (Numbers 13:16)

To check out a place or a situation beforehand is the modern equivalent of this biblical expression. Spies often have sinister reputations, but if we are to do our duty as Moses and his men did, we will also spy out the many lands God puts us into so we can do our best for Him. Remember that we are to be "wise as serpents, and harmless as doves" (Matthew 10:16).

stand in the gap

And I sought for a man among them, that should make up the hedge, and **stand in the gap** *before me for the land, that I should not destroy it: but I found none.* (Ezekiel 22:30)

Someone who can take up the slack and alleviate a problem that others can't is said to "stand in the gap." God was looking for such a man to "step up to the plate" as we say, but God could find none that would cause Him to appease His intended wrath against Israel.

The heart of the gospel shows itself here, for Jesus is the only Man that could actually stand in the gap that separated humankind and God—the gap of sin and its payment that had to be met. Jesus not only stood in the gap, but He closed it as well, allowing all people to now come to the throne of grace and find "help in time of need."

stand or fall by something

Who art thou that judgest another man's servant? to his own master he **standeth or falleth**. *Yea, he shall be holden up: for God is able to make him stand.* (Romans 14:4)

"Do or die," "make it or break it," "stand or fall"—each phrase has essentially the same meaning. They all refer to someone who is putting his or her reputation on the line in the effort to accomplish some goal.

The Bible here is talking about how we answer to our masters (supervisors) and those in authority over us. We stand or fall before our leaders just as we do before God.

stone's throw

And he was withdrawn from them about **a stone's cast**, *and kneeled down, and prayed.* (Luke 22:41)

Jesus was a short distance, or stone's throw, away from His disciples just before Judas arrived and gave Him the infamous "kiss of death" (see **kiss of death** in Appendix B). This is also the incident where Jesus "sweated blood" (see **sweat blood**).

Despite our modern measurements, we still say something is a "stone's throw" away (about 50– 75 yards).

straight and narrow

Because **strait** *is the gate,* **and narrow** *is the way, which leadeth unto life, and few there be that find it.* (Matthew 7:14)

To live a virtuous life constitutes walking the straight and narrow path. God's way is found only on the narrow way, not the broad way, and "few there be that find it."

In the days of Noah, the entire population of the world produced only one righteous man and his family. God said to Noah in Genesis 7:1: ". . . thee have I seen righteous before me in this generation," meaning the rest of the world was corrupt and would die in the flood since no others (besides Noah's family) were allowed on the boat.

Jesus said the last days would be similar to the days of Noah (Matthew 24:37), so we can expect fewer and fewer righteous people on the earth as we come closer and closer to Christ's return.

straining at gnats

Ye blind guides, which **strain at a gnat,** *and swallow a camel.*
(Matthew 23:24)

A major characteristic of a Pharisee is his insistence on being
what is called a "gnat-strainer"—one who harps on insignificant
matters to the neglect of the more serious. "Straining at gnats" is
an apt description, for to see a gnat, you do indeed have to strain
your eyes. To see the trivial faults of others requires the same.

There are those who will use this Scripture to preach against
all judgment of another's sin, but this is an incorrect application of
the teaching. Jesus didn't condemn pointing out another's sin, but
he did say to remove the "beam" out of your own eye first; then,
you will see clearly to remove the "mote" out of your brother's.

stumbling block

But we preach Christ crucified, unto the Jews a **stumblingblock,** *and
unto the Greeks foolishness;* (1 Corinthians 1:23)

The word "stumbling block" means just what it sounds like—
something that causes us to stumble or hinders our progress. Interestingly, one of the names given to Jesus is "stumbling block."
Indeed, He is a stumbling block, for in order to get past Him, one
has to die to self and his or her sins.

Stumbling causes us to go to our knees, and this is precisely
where we need to be in order to make progress in our Christian
walk. Forward progress by repeated stumbling may not make a
lot of sense, but a baby doesn't learn to walk without it.

suffer fools gladly

For ye **suffer fools gladly,** *seeing ye yourselves are wise.* (2 Corinthians 11:19)

Having patience with those who are less intelligent than us puts us in the group of those who "suffer fools gladly." Paul asked the Corinthian church to bear with him like they did when they suffered other fools gladly. Paul desired to instruct them in some areas they might have considered foolish, warning them that they could be deceived into accepting "another Jesus" and "another gospel" (v. 4).

Just mention the name "Jesus," and most people have some preconceived ideals associated with that name. But which Jesus is being talked about is another story altogether. There are many Jesus impostors, and it is our job to find and proclaim the real Jesus while "suffering fools gladly" who don't.

sweat blood

And being in an agony he prayed more earnestly: and his **sweat** *was as it were great drops of* **blood** *falling down to the ground.* (Luke 22:44)

Working extremely hard or "sweating blood" is found in the account of Jesus praying at the Mount of Olives. Scriptures state that Jesus prayed so fervently that His sweat "was as it were great drops of blood." The careful reader will notice that it didn't say He "sweated blood," only that His sweat was "as" blood.

Nonetheless, praying till you sweat in that manner is highly commendable, for the "effectual fervent prayer of a righteous man availeth much (James 5:16).

T

take it easy

And I will say to my soul, Soul, thou hast much goods laid up for many years; __take thine ease__, *eat, drink, and be merry.* (Luke 12:19)

Almost as popular as "goodbye," the expression "take it easy" was, in so many words, the utterance of the rich man in this parable recorded in Luke. The rich man thought he could slack off and "take it easy" because of his accumulated wealth. He also said he wanted to "eat, drink, and be merry," so these phrases have a lot in common.

The Eagles further popularized this expression in the 1970s with their song "Take It Easy." The philosophy of the world is to "take it easy," but God never told anyone to take it easy. Every time this expression is used in Scripture, it is used in the negative light of slothfulness. David, for example, speaks of the wicked and describes them as "at ease in Zion." From God's perspective, then, we may not want to "take it easy."

take the Lord's name in vain

Thou shalt not take the name of the LORD thy God in vain; for the LORD will not hold him guiltless that __taketh his name in vain__. (Exodus 20:7)

One of the Ten Commandments that is most misunderstood has to be this one from the book of Exodus. Popular misconception states that the expression "taking the Lord's name in vain" means using the name of God haphazardly or in exclamation. That is far from its intended application.

"Taking the Lord's name in vain" means just what it says: actually taking on the name of the Lord for our own benefit without really believing in Him in the first place. It is a vain exercise. False religion and its believers are guilty of breaking this commandment on a regular basis.

take under your wing

O Jerusalem, Jerusalem, thou that killest the prophets, and stonest them which are sent unto thee, how often would I have gathered thy children together, even as a hen **gathereth** *her chickens* **under her wings***, and ye would not!* (Matthew 23:37)

"Taking under your wing" indicates that you like someone enough to take care of, teach, and nourish that person, if need be. Jesus demonstrates His love for us by comparing what a hen does to its chicks and what He does for His children. David echoed this sentiment by saying in the Psalms, ". . . hide me under the shadow of thy wings" (Psalms 17:8).

take your breath away

Thou hidest thy face, they are troubled: thou **takest away their breath**, they die, and return to their dust. (Psalms 104:29)

Something that is breathtaking is usually a splendid sight or fabulous occurrence. The real breath taker is the Lord Himself who actually does, according to the Bible, "take your breath away" when you die. In the beginning, God breathed into Adam, and he "became a living soul." When we die, the Bible says God takes away our breath.

To be breathtaking, then, is not always a good thing. God is breathtaking literally and figuratively, for His looks are breathtaking as well as His actions.

tell it like it is

How hast thou counselled him that hath no wisdom? and how hast thou plentifully **declared the thing as it is**? (Job 26:3)

Howard Cosell's autobiography *Tell It Like It Is* demonstrated Howard's penchant for not holding anything back in his opinions on sports and its celebrities. When you "tell it like it is," you don't mince words or sugarcoat anything, and that's the way God likes it.

Christians should not hesitate in telling it like it is, for the gospel will always offend. If it doesn't, then perhaps we're watering it down with niceties.

Jesus offended people everywhere He went. Even the world acknowledges, "Sometimes, the truth hurts."

tender mercies (leave to one's)

Remember, O LORD, thy **tender mercies** *and thy lovingkindnesses; for they have been ever of old.* (Psalm 25:6)

Today, we facetiously say we leave someone to another's tender mercies when we leave that person in the care of another who isn't so appealing for one reason or another. "Tender mercies" takes on a different meaning in Scripture, signifying God's literal mercy on us.

The term "tender mercies" shows up as the title of a 1983 movie starring Robert Duvall, but this movie title had nothing to do with God's mercy. Movie producers and writers often find it increasingly appealing to use the Bible as a source for their production titles. (see appendices C and D for a complete listing of motion picture and song titles that contain biblical expressions).

their name is legion

And he asked him, What is thy name? And he answered, saying, **My name is Legion:** *for we are many.* (Mark 5:9)

You hear this phrase used often to denote those whose accomplishments are legendary or famous. The word "legion" is currently used to describe a multitude or host, and this is how it is used in the Bible. In this account, Jesus cast out devils (demons) who called themselves "Legion" and sent them into a herd of swine.

Does this mean that animals can be possessed? They were in this instance, and Satan most certainly uses animals for his purposes. The warning, "Beware of dogs," takes on new significance, doesn't it?

there but for the grace of God go I

But by the grace of God I am what I am: and his grace which *was bestowed* upon me was not in vain; but I labored more abundantly than they all: yet not I, but the grace of God which was with me. (1 Corinthians 15:10)

Paul recounted his past by stating he persecuted the church of God heavily before his conversion. The expression "by the grace of God" is used often by those who have had some particular downfall in their lives and were helped by God in their time of need.

God's grace is truly amazing, for the only real difference between a sinner and a saint is God's grace. Every saint can say, "There but for the grace of God go I" when he speaks of what might have happened to him had he followed the crowds and not the way of God. We should never reach the point of pride where we can't acknowledge as the hymn says that God "saved a wretch like me."

there's a time for everything

To every thing there is a season, and **a time to every purpose** *under the heaven:* (Ecclesiastes 3:1)

We hear people say, "There's a time for everything," yet they don't realize where that statement originates. King Solomon penned this in Ecclesiastes long before the group, The Byrds, sang about it. Solomon says there are appropriate times for many things: a "time to love, and a time to hate"; a "time to kill, and a time to heal."

Hating and killing won't be well received with the "I don't hate anyone or kill anything" crowd. Logically thinking, it is impossible to love everybody and everything. True love hates evil; it hates everything that destroys true love. We can't love the truth and love a lie at the same time.

thorn in my side

And lest I should be exalted above measure through the abundance of the revelations, there was given to me **a thorn in the flesh,** *the messenger of Satan to buffet me, lest I should be exalted above measure.* (2 Corinthians 12:7)

Each of us usually has something we can point to as a "thorn in our side." This is a commonly spoken phrase representing a constant irritant that could be mental, emotional, or physical. The apostle Paul mentioned that God gave him a "thorn" in order for Paul not to be "exalted above measure" or, in other words, to humble him.

Paul's thorn was a big one—a "messenger of Satan" to "buffet" him. Who this "messenger of Satan" was the Scriptures do not say. Most of us should be thankful that our thorns aren't as sharp as Paul's "thorn in the side."

through a glass darkly

For now we see **through a glass, darkly**; *but then face to face: now I know in part, but then shall I know even as also I am known.* (1 Corinthians 13:12)

The biblical expression "through a glass darkly" describes how we don't see the spiritual world clearly at the present time. When we are changed and enter into heaven, then we will "know even also as I am known," said Paul.

The Bible does say that "Eye hath not seen, nor ear heard, neither have entered into the heart of man, the things which God hath prepared for them that love him" (1 Corinthians 2:9).

tomorrow will take care of itself

Take therefore no thought for the morrow: for **the morrow shall take thought** *for the things* **of itself.** *Sufficient unto the day is the evil thereof.* (Matthew 6:34)

From time to time, we all get caught up in worrying about the future. Jesus knew this and instructed us to "take therefore no thought for the morrow." The future is in His hands, not ours, and that is the reason we don't need to worry about next week, next year, or any other time in the future.

Many professional athletes talk about taking their season "one game at a time" when discussing their chances of winning or getting in the playoffs. Jesus would agree with that mentality of taking one day at a time because He said, "Sufficient unto the day *is* the evil thereof."

Tomorrow doesn't take care of itself without the Lord directing it. Christians realize this, but the world likes to use this expression as if tomorrow had a mind of its own.

toss and turn

He will surely violently **turn and toss** *thee like a ball into a large country: there shalt thou die, and there the chariots of thy glory shall be the shame of thy lord's house.* (Isaiah 22:18)

After a bad night's sleep, we might say that we "tossed and turned." The Bible's use of this phrase doesn't involve a bad night's sleep. The Lord was pronouncing judgment on a certain Shebna, a treasurer of the Persians, for his invasion of Israel. God said He would "turn and toss" him like a ball.

turn the other cheek

But I say unto you, That ye resist not evil: but whosoever shall smite thee on thy right **cheek, turn to him the other also.** (Matthew 5:39)

All of us probably remember when we were children and some schoolyard bully slapped or punched us in the face. Our normal response was to hit back at the bully. Turning the other cheek never entered our minds.

"Turning the other cheek," in the literal sense, is not the easiest thing to do, but it is a commandment of the Lord. Jesus did this very thing when He was struck on the face by His enemies.

We apply this expression to non-violent matters also, telling others to "turn the other cheek" and not to seek revenge when someone does something to them that upsets them.

two-edged sword (double-edged)

For the word of God is quick, and powerful, and sharper than any **two-edged sword,** *piercing even to the dividing asunder of soul and spirit, and of the joints and marrow, and is a discerner of the thoughts and intents of the heart.* (Hebrews 4:12)

A "double-edged sword" is anything that produces both good and bad effects simultaneously. There could be no better example of a double-edged sword than the Bible, for it cuts to the heart like a sword and will either save your soul and change your heart or condemn your soul and harden your heart.

One reason the Bible is avoided by so many is that it reveals to us our own "thoughts and intents." It reaches into the very recesses of our souls and makes us face our real selves, and that's not a pretty sight.

two heads are better than one

<u>Two are better than one</u>; *because they have a good reward for their labor.* (Ecclesiastes 4:9)

Anybody working on a project knows that it's usually a good idea to have the opinion of others to help us make a decision. One head (our own) is not good enough, and that is the meaning of this expression.

Ecclesiastes 4:9 probably refers to the subject of marriage and how "two heads are better than one" when it comes to coping together with life's problems.

U

under the sun

So I returned, and considered all the oppressions that are done <u>under</u> <u>the sun</u>: *and behold the tears of such as were oppressed, and they had no comforter; and on the side of their oppressors there was power; but they had no comforter.* (Ecclesiastes 4:1)

Instead of saying "all" of something, we might say "everything under the sun" because that would include just about anything.

Jesus, interestingly enough, is called the "Sun of Righteousness" in Malachi 4:2 (that's "*Sun*" with a "*u*"). Actually, Jesus and the sun have a lot in common. Both have risen in the East, and both give light and life. There are many more parallels to God in nature and in the heavens, for "The heavens declare the glory of God" as it says in Psalm 19:1.

V

various and sundry ways

God, who at <u>sundry times and in divers manners</u>, *spake in time past unto the fathers by the prophets.* (Hebrews 1:1)

God has always used a variety of ways to speak. He speaks through prophets, angels, dreams, donkeys, His enemies, and lastly, His Son. God speaks to us today through the Bible: "But the word is very nigh thee, in thy mouth, and in thy heart, that thou mayest do it."

voice in the wilderness

The <u>voice</u> *of him that crieth* <u>in the wilderness</u>, *Prepare ye the way of the* Lord, *make straight in the desert a highway for our God.* (Isaiah 40:3)

"A voice in the wilderness" is anyone that is perceived as a lone protester with very little support. John the Baptist was the original voice in the wilderness who cried out about the coming Messiah and how He would change the hearts of those who would follow Him.

Every prophet of God has been a voice in the wilderness. Every Christian should be a "voice in the wilderness" proclaiming the truth of God's ways.

W-Z

wages of sin

*For **the wages of sin** is death: but the gift of God is eternal life through Jesus Christ our Lord.* (Romans 6:23)

Everything has its price, and sin is no exception. It just so happens that the "wages of sin," that is, the consequence or price of sin, is the most expensive we will ever encounter—eternal punishment. Sin exacts heavy wages which we can never fully repay. Jesus, however, paid the price that was accepted by God, for the price was the blood of God Himself in the person of Jesus Christ.

Each of us must make the decision as to who wil pay off the debt. Will we try to pay it off our ourselves or accept the fact that Jesus has already paid the debt?

wash your hands of something

*When Pilate saw that he could not prevail, but that rather a tumult was made, he took water, and **washed his hands** before the multitude, saying, I am innocent of the blood of this just person: see ye to it.* (Matthew 27:24)

"Washing your hands" of a matter says that you are no longer taking any responsibility for a situation and are pronouncing yourself clear of any accountability to it. Pilate refused to take part in sending Jesus to the cross. However, as he was under immense pressure to allow Jesus to be crucified, he reluctantly turned Jesus over to the multitudes who crucified Him anyway.

Refusing to make a decision about Jesus occurs on the individual level as well, but washing our hands of the Lord doesn't exonerate us. Jesus said, "He that is not with me is against me."

weaker vessel

Likewise, ye husbands, dwell with them according to knowledge, giving honor unto the wife, as unto the <u>weaker vessel</u>, and as being heirs together of the grace of life; that your prayers be not hindered. (1 Peter 3:7)

As you might expect, this is not a particularly popular expression with the feminist movement today. Though women are a "weaker vessel" compared to men, this does not mean that a woman is somehow less of a person or less important than a man; it's just that women and men have different roles to fulfill.

Though a woman is classified as a weaker vessel, any man can verify that a woman has certain strengths that can't be equaled by man. The ironic thing is that she has the ability to make man a weaker vessel and does so on a regular basis.

weighed in the balance (weighed and wanting)

TEKEL; Thou art <u>weighed in the balances</u>, and art found wanting. (Daniel 5:27)

The "writing on the wall" incident (see **writing on the wall**), where God's hand appeared and wrote on a wall during a big party that King Belshazzar threw is the context of the biblical expression "weighed and wanting." The message that God wrote on the wall translated into English included the words "weighed in the balance."

Today, this expression speaks of the deficiencies of an individual or group and how such deficiencies relate to the matter at hand. Those who think God will actually weigh our deeds will come up "weighed and wanting." None of our deeds are sufficient without belief in God.

what have we here?

Now therefore, __what have I here__, saith the LORD, that my people is taken away for nought? they that rule over them make them to howl, saith the LORD; and my name continually every day is blasphemed. (Isaiah 52:5)

We hear this rhetorical question asked when someone discovers something of significance or surprise. God Himself used it when musing over Israel's captivity by another nation. Of course, it wasn't a surprise to God, but it showed some of the personality of God through His use of rhetorical language.

wheels within wheels

The appearance of the wheels and their work was like unto the color of a beryl: and they four had one likeness: and their appearance and their work was as it were a __wheel in the middle of a wheel__. (Ezekiel 1:16)

"Wheels within wheels" is a picturesque illustration of the complexity of a situation which isn't readily apparent to those on the outside. Literally speaking, "wheels within wheels" depicts the operations of modern clocks, transmissions, and other mechanical inventions.

Ezekiel's visions of living creatures appeared to him as "wheels within wheels," not only for what they looked like, but also how they operated together.

It's also an excellent analogy of the operations of God in our lives, for He does things for a multitude of reasons and purposes that we don't always understand, but we eventually see that He runs His show "like a well-oiled machine."

when the spirit moves you

And the <u>**Spirit of the Lord began to move him**</u> *at times in the camp of Dan between Zorah and Eshtaol.* (Judges 13:25)

Telling people to act "whenever the spirit moves you" indicates that we are permitting them to do things whenever they feel like it. The Bible doesn't use this cliché figuratively but applies it to Samuel and how the Spirit of God really did begin to move him as a child.

wise in your own eyes

Woe unto them that are <u>**wise in their own eyes,**</u> *and prudent in their own sight!* (Isaiah 5:21)

Being "wise in your own eyes" is a little more serious than at first glance. God pronounced woe on those who are "wise in their own eyes," and when God says "woe," it means trouble and anguish is not far away. This expression is descriptive of those whose wisdom is based on their own opinion of themselves.

What we think of ourselves is of little concern to God, but very important to the average person! Self-esteem is the mantra for the day, but God never told us to esteem ourselves. In fact, we are to esteem others higher than ourselves only because we naturally esteem ourselves in the flesh. What we are to esteem are His words more than our necessary food (Job 23:12).

If our wisdom is based on ourselves, how vain and empty is that? According to Proverbs 1:7, "The fear of the LORD *is* the beginning of knowledge: *but* fools despise wisdom and instruction."

with a vengeance

Say to them that are of a fearful heart, Be strong, fear not: behold, your God will come **with vengeance,** *even God with a recompence; he will come and save you.* (Isaiah 35:4)

Acting with a vengeance denotes actions that are hard, swift, sure, and determined. Another biblical quote involving vengeance has God saying, "Vengeance is mine, I will repay" (Romans 12:19 [cf. Deuteronomy 32:35, 41; Psalm 94:1]).

God will certainly repay the wicked and dreadfully so. When the Lord returns, His wrath will be severe. The book of Isaiah says the Lord's garments will be soaked with the blood of the unrighteous: "Wherefore *art thou* red in thine apparel, and thy garments like him that treadeth in the winefat? I have trodden the winepress alone; and of the people *there was* none with me: for I will tread them in mine anger, and trample them in my fury; and their blood shall be sprinkled upon my garments, and I will stain all my raiment" (Isaiah 63:2–3).

Surprisingly, this ghastly account is what is being referred to in the famous "Battle Hymn of the Republic" song: "He is trampling out the vintage where the grapes of wrath are stored/He hath loosed the fateful lightning of His terrible swift sword:/His truth is marching on."

Most people sing this without realizing that they're singing about God systematically destroying the wicked when He returns.

with you in spirit

For though I be absent in the flesh, yet am I **with you in** *the* **spirit,** *joying and beholding your order, and the steadfastness of your faith in Christ.* (Colossians 2:5)

To be with someone "in spirit" is to be with that person in thoughts when we can't be with that person physically.

When a Christian says he is "with us in spirit," he can literally mean it, for each Christian has the same spirit of God in him or her. Because all believers are in the Holy Spirit (who is omnipresent), they are with each other in spirit as well.

woe is me!

Woe is me, *that I sojourn in Mesech, that I dwell in the tents of Kedar!* (Psalm 120:5)

David lamented his troubles and gloom by exclaiming the adage, "Woe is me." Jesus throughout the Gospels proclaimed "Woe unto you" when speaking unto the wicked and the Pharisees. "Woe unto you," of course, means calamity and doom is on the way.

wolf in sheep's clothing

Beware of false prophets, which come to you **in sheep's clothing,** *but inwardly they are ravening* **wolves.** (Matthew 7:15)

Jesus warned His followers of "wolves in sheep's clothing" who, in reality, were false prophets pretending to be ministers of the gospel.

A child of God should be able to recognize these charlatans because Jesus said, "My sheep hear my voice, and I know them, and they follow me" (John 10:27). Anyone can recognize a wolf; it's the wolf in sheep's clothing of whom we need to be wary.

won't lift a finger

For they bind heavy burdens and grievous to be borne, and lay them on men's shoulders; but they themselves **will not move them with one of their fingers.** (Matthew 23:4)

This was another in a long line of railing accusations against the Pharisees. Jesus said they wouldn't "move . . . one of their fingers" to help others. Pharisaic people love to talk about their concern for the unfortunate, but when it comes down to actually doing something, that spirit of kindness somehow disappears or is masqueraded behind an act of kindness for some devious purpose.

word is gone out

I have sworn by myself, **the word is gone out** *of my mouth in righteousness, and shall not return, That unto me every knee shall bow, every tongue shall swear.* (Isaiah 45:23)

When we say, "the word has gone out," we refer to a matter being made known to the masses. The word of God has literally gone out to all the world. God used His people and didn't need a slick marketing campaign to get it done.

The God of the Old Testament who said every knee would bow to Him is the same God in the New Testament (Philippians 2:10) to whom every knee will also bow: "That at the name of Jesus every knee should bow, of *things* in heaven, and *things* in earth, and *things* under the earth."

writing on the wall

In the same hour came forth fingers of a man's hand, and **wrote** *over against the candlestick* **upon the plaister of the wall** *of the king's palace: and the king saw the part of the hand that wrote.* (Daniel 5:5)

Can't you just see the big party King Belshazzar was throwing? Everyone was getting drunk (drinking from vessels from the Hebrew Temple) and living it up. Suddenly, a hand appears out of nowhere and starts writing on the wall. It was a message to the king that his life had been judged and was found quite lacking.

According to the Bible, the king was so scared his knees started shaking.

"Writing on the wall" refers to the inevitable, unfortunate circumstances that await an individual. When the individual recognizes what's about to occur, he sees "the writing on the wall." Employees about to lose their jobs often say, "I saw the handwriting on the wall." As Christians, we need keep our eyes and ears open for what the Lord is saying to us.

written in stone

But if the ministration of death, **written** *and engraven* **in stones,** *was glorious, so that the children of Israel could not steadfastly behold the face of Moses for the glory of his countenance; which glory was to be done away: How shall not the ministration of the spirit be rather glorious?* (2 Corinthians 3:7–8)

If plans aren't written in stone, we assume they aren't finalized, or at least they can be altered. The world loves to alter and amend its written codes. Though it is difficult to amend our U.S. Constitution, it has happened twenty-seven times.

When God gave the Ten Commandments written in stone, He was showing us the permanency of the Word of God and its need for no alterations whatsoever. The Bible should be treated as if every page were written in stone! It should not be altered or amended.

You can't take it with you

For we brought nothing into this world, and it is certain **we can carry nothing out.** (1 Timothy 6:7)

All our possessions and all our worldly accomplishments will not follow us into heaven. We do come "full circle" back to where we started—with nothing. We were born with nothing, not even clothes on our back. And nothing is exactly what we will take with us when we leave this earth.

There is something intangible, however, you can take with you, and that is whatever works you have done for the Lord. In 1 Corinthians 3:13–14, it states, "Every man's work shall be made manifest: for the day shall declare it, because it shall be revealed by fire; and the fire shall try every man's work of what sort it is. If any man's work abide which he hath built thereupon, he shall receive a reward."

Our life "down here" will determine our rewards "up there." Our labor is not in vain, for one day we will reap the benefits of our godly deeds. As some have said, "It's hard work, but the benefits are 'out of this world.' "

you're the man!

And Nathan said to David, **Thou art the man***. Thus saith the* LORD *God of Israel, I annointed thee king over Israel, and I delivered thee out of the hand of Saul.* (2 Samuel 12:7)

Nathan the prophet had just finished telling David a parable of a rich man and a poor man—the poor man having but an ewe lamb. In the story, the rich man steals the poor man's one and only lamb in order to feed one of his guests. David, not knowing that Nathan was speaking figuratively, grew very angry and demanded that justice be served for such an act of thievery. Nathan then told David that he, David, was "the man" who represented the thief in his story.

So Nathan's parable was true—David had taken another man's lone lamb (Bathsheba). In an effort to cover up his sinful act of adultery, King David brought Bathsheba's husband (Uriah) home from the battle so that Uriah would sleep with her. Uriah, as a good soldier, refused to sleep with his wife. Since this devious plan didn't work, David made further plans to cover up his sin. He made certain that Uriah was moved to the frontlines of the battle where he would be killed—and he was.

The phrase "you are the man" or the abbreviated version "you da' man" indicates someone thinks another is a highly admirable person. In the Bible, the expression is a finger-pointing accusation towards an adulterous murderer.

Afterword

What has been dealt with to a large extent in this work is language, and in particular, the language of the King James Bible. According to Genesis 2:19, when Adam was created, he was already endued with the gift of language because he had the ability to give names to all the animals. Because Adam was the only human on the planet (talk about lonely!), he did not learn language from anyone but God. Thus, man did not invent language according to the Bible. God gave man a language to speak and the ability to learn it. From Adam through his descendants we all learned to communicate.

Since all the world spoke only one language until the Tower of Babel incident, we can also surmise that the characteristics of this one language were carried over into the other languages that God also created. If you remember, man did not invent other languages either, but God "did there confound the language of all the earth" (Genesis 11:9).

The existence of all the world's languages is one of the greatest proofs of the existence of God as mentioned earlier in this work. The fact that God was and still is very involved in our use and style of language has been a theme promulgated throughout this work.

As He did with Adam, God is still teaching us language today through the Bible's numerous quaint and colorful expressions. Let us rejoice as King David did when he said the following: "Princes have persecuted me without a cause: but my heart standeth in awe of thy word. I rejoice at thy word, as one that findeth great spoil" (Psalm 119:161–2). The Bible is an inexhaustible treasure that most of the world has yet to fully discover.

Appendix A
Once Popular Expressions
Used Less Frequently Today

abomination of desolation

(a detestable thing)

When ye therefore shall see <u>the abomination of desolation</u>, *spoken of by Daniel the prophet, stand in the holy place, (whoso readeth, let him understand).* (Matthew 24:16)

Abraham's bosom

(paradise, heaven, or bliss)

And it came to pass, that the beggar died, and was carried by the angels into <u>Abraham's bosom</u>*: the rich man also died, and was buried.* (Luke 16:22)

Ancient of Days

(another name for Jesus)

I beheld till the thrones were cast down, and <u>the Ancient of days</u> *did sit, whose garment was white as snow, and the hair of his head like the pure wool: his throne was like the fiery flame, and his wheels as burning fire.* (Daniel 7:9)

answer a fool according to his foolishness

(give a foolish answer to a fool)

<u>Answer a fool according to his</u> *folly, lest he be wise in his own conceit.* (Proverbs 26:5)

as one man

(people acting in unison)

And all the people arose **as one man,** *saying, We will not any of us go to his tent, neither will we any of us turn into his house.* (Judges 20:8)

ask for bread and receive a stone

(to get much less than requested)

Or what man is there of you, whom if his son **ask bread, will he give him a stone?** (Matthew 7:9)

balm in Gilead

(something soothing; relief)

Is there no **balm in Gilead;** *is there no physician there? why then is not the health of the daughter of my people recovered?* (Jeremiah 8:22)

beard the lion

(confront a dangerous situation)

And I went out after him, and smote him, and delivered it out of his mouth: and when he arose against me, I **caught him by his beard,** *and smote him, and slew him.* (1 Samuel 17:35)

bear false witness

(lie or deceive)

He saith unto him, Which? Jesus said, Thou shalt do no murder, Thou shalt not commit adultery, Thou shalt not steal, Thou shalt not **bear false witness.** (Matthew 19:18)

before the flood

(ancient times; a long time ago)

And Joshua said unto all the people, Thus saith the LORD *God of Israel, Your fathers dwelt on* **the other side of the flood** *in old time, even*

Terah, the father of Abraham, and the father of Nachor: and they served other gods. (Joshua 24:2)

be of good cheer

(happy and content)

These things have I spoken unto you, that in me ye might have peace. In the world ye shall have tribulation: but **be of good cheer;** *I have overcome the world.* (John 16:33)

bound hand and foot

(tied up at the hands and feet)

And he that was dead came forth, **bound hand and foot** *with grave-clothes and his face was bound about with a napkin. Jesus saith unto them, Loose him, and let him go.* (John 11:44)

broken reed

(an unreliable person or thing)

Lo, thou trustest in the staff of this **broken reed,** *on Egypt; whereon if a man lean, it will go into his hand, and pierce it: so is Pharaoh king of Egypt to all that trust in him.* (Isaiah 36:6)

camel through the eye of a needle

(an obvious impossibility)

And again I say unto you, It is easier for **a camel to go through the eye of a needle,** *than for a rich man to enter into the kingdom of God.* (Matthew 19:24)

cast into outer darkness

(banished, shut out)

But the children of the kingdom shall be **cast out into outer darkness:** *there shall be weeping and gnashing of teeth.* (Matthew 8:12)

cast out devils
(to change a person's evil ways)

Many will say to me in that day, Lord, Lord, have we not prophesied in thy name? and in thy name have <u>cast out devils</u>? *and in thy name done many wonderful works?* (Matthew 7:22)

cast pearls before swine
(offering to others who don't appreciate it)

Give not that which is holy unto the dogs, neither <u>cast ye your pearls before swine,</u> *lest they trample them under their feet, and turn again and rend you.* (Matthew 7:6)

cast your bread upon the waters
(to take a chance through investment)

<u>Cast</u> *thy* <u>bread upon the waters,</u> *for thou shalt find it after many days.* (Ecclesiastes 11:1)

child of the devil
(an evil person)

And said, O full of all subtilty and all mischief, thou <u>child of the devil,</u> *thou enemy of all righteousness, wilt thou not cease to pervert the right ways of the Lord?* (Acts 13:10)

children of this world
(the unsaved masses; heathen)

And the lord commended the unjust steward, because he had done wisely: for <u>the children of this world</u> *are in their generation wiser than the children of light.* (Luke 16:8)

citizen of no mean city
(a resident of a well-known city)

But Paul said, I am a man which am a Jew of Tarsus, a city in Cilicia, **a citizen of no mean city***: and, I beseech thee, suffer me to speak unto the people.* (Acts 21:39)

cloud no bigger than a man's hand
(an omen or warning)

And it came to pass at the seventh time, that he said, Behold, there ariseth **a little cloud** *out of the sea,* **like a man's hand***. And he said, Go up, say unto Ahab, Prepare thy chariot, and get thee down, that the rain stop thee not.* (1 Kings 18:44)

cloud of witnesses
(a multitude of eyewitnesses)

Wherefore seeing we also are compassed about with so great **a cloud of witnesses***, let us lay aside every weight, and the sin which doth so easily beset us, and let us run with patience the race that is set before us.* (Hebrews 12:1)

cover a multitude of sins
(inclusive of many different items or ideas)

And above all things have fervent charity among yourselves: for charity shall **cover the multitude of sins***.* (1 Peter 4:8)

crown of glory
(an outstanding accomplishment)

And when the chief Shepherd shall appear, ye shall receive **a crown of glory** *that fadeth not away.* (1 Peter 5:4)

daily bread
(one's physical needs)

Give us this day our **daily bread***.* (Matthew 6:11)

darken counsel

(cloud the issue or prevent dialogue)

Who is this **darkeneth counsel** *by words without knowledge?* (Job 38:2)

deaf as an adder

(not good of hearing)

Their poison is like the poison of a serpent: they are **like the deaf adder** *that stoppeth her ear.* (Psalm 58:4)

divide the spoils

(split up goods amongst others)

Thou hast multiplied the nation, and not increased the joy: they joy before thee according to the joy in harvest, and as men rejoice when they **divide the spoil.** (Isaiah 9:3)

draw a bow at a venture

(to take a chance at something)

And a certain man **drew a bow at a venture,** *and smote the king of Israel between the joints of the harness: therefore he said to his chariot man, Turn thine hand, that thou mayest carry me out of the host; for I am wounded.* (2 Chronicles 18:33)

enemy is at the gate

(trouble is near)

As arrows are in the hand of a mighty man; so are children of the youth. Happy is the man that hath his quiver full of them: they shall not be ashamed, but they shall speak with **the enemies in the gate**. (Psalm 127:5)

escape the bear and fall to the lion

(to go from bad to worse)

As if a man did <u>flee from a lion, and a bear met him;</u> *or went into the house, and leaned his hand on the wall, and a serpent bit him.* (Amos 5:19)

ewe lamb

(what one treasures the most)

But the poor man had nothing, save one little <u>ewe lamb</u>, *which he had bought and nourished up: and it grew up together with him, and with his children; it did eat of his own meat, and drank of his own cup, and lay in his bosom, and was unto him as a daughter.* (2 Samuel 12:3)

fallen angel

(someone who has morally degenerated)

How art thou <u>fallen from heaven, O Lucifer</u>, *son of the morning! how art thou cut down to the ground, which didst weaken the nations!* (Isaiah 14:12)

fall of a sparrow

(the importance of little things)

Are not two <u>sparrows</u> *sold for a farthing? and one of them shall not* <u>fall</u> *on the ground without your Father.* (Matthew 10:29)

fall on stony ground

(an idea that does not win acceptance or approval)

And some <u>fell on stony ground</u>, *where it had not much earth; and immediately it sprang up, because it had no depth of earth.* (Mark 4:5)

fear and trembling
(sarcastic apprehension or fright)

And his inward affection is more abundant toward you, whilst he remembereth the obedience of you all, how with **fear and trembling** *ye received him.* (2 Corinthians 7:15)

fearfully and wonderfully made
(anything of complex design)

I will praise thee; for I am **fearfully and wonderfully made**: *marvellous are thy works; and that my soul knoweth right well.* (Psalm 139:14)

flesh-pots of Egypt
(creature comforts that are missed)

And the children of Israel said unto them, Would to God we had died by the hand of the LORD in the land **of Egypt**, *when we sat* **by the flesh pots**, *and when we did eat bread to the full; for ye have brought us forth into this wilderness, to kill this whole assembly with hunger.* (Exodus 16:3)

fullness of time
(the appointed or right time)

But when **the fulness of the time** *was come, God sent forth his Son, made of a woman, made under the law.* (Galatians 4:4)

gall and wormwood
(a bitter experience to endure)

Remembering mine affliction and my misery, the **wormwood and the gall.** (Lamentations 3:19)

gathered to your fathers

(to die)

And also all that generation were **gathered unto their fathers***: and there arose another generation after them, which knew not the LORD, nor yet the works which he had done for Israel.* (Judges 2:10)

gift of tongues

(multilingual)

And God hath set some in the church, first apostles, secondarily prophets, thirdly teachers, after that miracles, then gifts of healings, helps, governments, **diversities of tongues***.* (1 Corinthians 12:28)

gird up your loins

(to get ready for strenuous work or action)

And Elisha the prophet called one of the children of the prophets, and said unto him, **Gird up thy loins***, and take this box of oil in thine hand, and go to Ramoth-gilead.* (2 Kings 9:1)

God and Mammon

(the choice between serving God and riches)

No man can serve two masters: for either he will hate the one, and love the other; or else he will hold to the one, and despise the other. Ye cannot serve **God and mammon***.* (Matthew 6:24)

good men and true

(reliable, honest people)

And, behold, there was a man named Joseph, a counselor; and he was **a good man, and a just.** (Luke 23:50)

greater love hath no man
(the greatest sacrifice you can make for another)

<u>Greater love hath no man</u> *than this, that a man lay down his life for his friends.* (John 15:13)

grind the face of someone
(to govern harshly)

What mean ye that ye beat my people to pieces, and <u>grind the faces of the poor</u>? *saith the Lord God of hosts.* (Isaiah 3:15)

hand against every man, one's
(the acts of criminals and rebels)

And he will be a wild man; his <u>hand will be against every man</u>, *and every man's hand against him; and he shall dwell in the presence of his brethren.* (Genesis 16:12)

hand has lost its cunning, one's
(skills are deteriorating)

If I forget thee, O Jerusalem, let my right <u>hand forget her cunning</u>. (Psalm 137:5)

have your feet on another's neck
(dominion over someone)

And it came to pass, when they brought out those kings unto Joshua, that Joshua called for all the men of Israel, and said unto the captains of the men of war which went with him, Come near, put your feet upon the necks of these kings. And they came near, and <u>put their feet upon the necks of them</u>. (Joshua 10:24)

heap coals of fire on one's head

(doing good to your enemies)

For thou shalt **heap coals of fire upon his head**, *and the* LORD *shall reward thee.* (Proverbs 25:22)

hewers of wood and drawers of water

(lowest level workers)

And the princes said unto them, Let them live; but let them be **hewers of wood and drawers of water** *unto all the congregation; as the princes had promised them.* (Joshua 9:21)

hide your light under a bushel

(conceal one's abilities out of modesty)

Neither do men **light** *a candle, and* **put it under a bushel**, *but on a candlestick; and it giveth light unto all that are in the house.* (Matthew 5:15)

hope deferred

(when one's hopes and dreams are delayed)

Hope deferred *maketh the heart sick: but when the desire cometh, it is a tree of life.* (Proverbs 13:12)

howling wilderness

(a scary place or situation)

He found him in a desert land, and in the waste **howling wilderness**; *he led him about, he instructed him, he kept him as the apple of his eye.* (Deuteronomy 32:10)

inner man

(the soul; the real personality)

That he would grant you, according to the riches of his glory, to be strengthened with might by his Spirit in **the inner man.** (Ephesians 3:16)

jot or tittle

(the smallest amount; nothing)

For verily I say unto you, Till heaven and earth pass, **one jot or one tittle** *shall in no wise pass from the law, till all be fulfilled.* (Matthew 5:18)

joy cometh in the morning

(blessing comes after suffering)

For his anger endureth but a moment; in hi favour is life: weeping may endure for a night, but **joy cometh in the morning.** (Psalm 30:5)

kick against the pricks

(to rebel and not face the truth)

And he said, Who art thou, Lord? And the Lord said, I am Jesus whom thou persecutest: it is hard for thee **to kick against the pricks.** (Acts 9:5)

king of terrors

(death personified)

His confidence shall be rooted out of his tabernacle, and it shall bring him to **the king of terrors.** (Job 18:14)

laborer is worthy of his hire

(a worker deserves his wages)

And in the same house remain, eating and drinking such things as they give: for **the laborer is worthy of his hire**. *Go not from house to house.* (Luke 10:7)

land of Nod

(a state of deep sleep)

And Cain went out from the presence of the LORD, and dwelt in **the land of Nod,** *on the east of Eden.* (Genesis 4:16)

law of the Medes and Persians

(that which can't be changed)

Now, O king, establish the decree, and sign the writing, that it be not changed, according to **the law of the Medes and Persians,** *which altereth not.* (Daniel 6:8)

length and breadth of the land, through

(the whole land)

Arise, walk through **the land in the length of it and in the breadth** *of it; for I will give it unto thee.* (Genesis 13:17)

let the dead bury their dead

(let others do their own business)

But Jesus said unto him, Follow me; and **let the dead bury their dead.** (Matthew 8:22)

lighten one's darkness

(to cheer up and encourage)

For thou art my lamp, O LORD: and the LORD will **lighten my darkness.**
(2 Samuel 22:29)

like a lamb to the slaughter
(go quietly in the face of punishment)

He was oppressed, and he was afflicted, yet he opened not his mouth: he is brought **as a lamb to the slaughter,** *and as a sheep before her shearers is dumb, so he openeth not his mouth.* (Isaiah 53:7)

lion shall lie down with the lamb
(a future peace hoped for)

The wolf and the lamb shall feed together, *and the lion shall eat straw like the bullock: and dust shall be the serpent's meat. They shall not hurt nor destroy in all my holy mountain, saith the LORD.* (Isaiah 65:25)

loaves and fishes
(being religious for any monetary gain)

Then he took the five **loaves and the two fishes,** *and looking up to heaven, he blessed them, and brake, and gave to the disciples to set before the multitude.* (Luke 9:16)

look on the wine when it's red
(get drunk)

Look not thou upon the wine when it is red, *when it giveth his color in the cup, when it moveth itself aright.* (Proverbs 23:31)

make glad the heart of man
(help the heart)

And wine that <u>maketh glad the heart of man</u>, and oil to make his face to shine, and bread which strengtheneth man's heart. (Psalm 104:15)

mark of the beast

(an omen of evil)

And the beast was taken, and with him the false prophet that wrought miracles before him, with which he deceived them that had received <u>the mark of the beast</u>, and them that worshipped his image. These both were cast alive into a lake of fire burning with brimstone. (Revelation 19:20)

meek shall inherit the earth

(God's people will own the world)

But <u>the meek shall inherit the earth</u>; and shall delight themselves in the abundance of peace. (Psalm 37:11)

mote in the eye

(accusing others of faults that you have)

And why beholdest thou the <u>mote that is in thy brother's eye</u>, but considerest not the beam that is in thine own eye? (Matthew 7:3)

move and have your being

(living or existing somewhere)

For in him we <u>live, and move, and have our being</u>; as certain also of your own poets have said, For we are also his offspring. (Acts 17:28)

nail someone to the cross

(prove, accuse, or punish another)

Blotting out the handwriting of ordinances that was against us, which was contrary to us, and took it out of the way, __nailing to his cross__. (Colossians 2:14)

no respecter of persons

(to give no special treatment to anyone)

Then Peter opened his mouth, and said, Of a truth I perceive that God is __no respecter of persons__. (Acts 10:34)

of the earth, earthy

(physical, material)

The first man is __of the earth, earthy__: the second man is the Lord from heaven. (1 Corinthians 15:47)

old Adam

(corrupt human nature)

Knowing this, that our __old man__ is crucified with him, that the body of sin might be destroyed, that henceforth we should not serve sin. (Romans 6:6)

old wine into new bottles

(putting a new package on old material)

And no man putteth __new wine into old bottles__: else the new wine doth burst the bottles, and the wine is spilled, and the bottles will be marred: but new wine must be put into new bottles. (Mark 2:22)

one flesh

(united in marriage)

What? know ye not that he which is joined to an harlot is one body? for two, saith he, shall be **one flesh**. (1 Corinthians 6:16)

peace that passeth all understanding
(peace of mind)

And the **peace of God, which passeth all understanding**, *shall keep your hearts and minds through Christ Jesus.* (Philippians 4:7)

Physician, heal thyself
(take care of your own problems)

And he said unto them, Ye will surely say unto me this proverb, **Physician, heal thyself**: *whatsoever we have heard done in Capernaum, do also here in thy country.* (Luke 4:23)

possess your soul in patience
(to be long-suffering)

In your patience **possess ye your souls.** (Luke 21:19)

powers of darkness
(evil, satanic authority)

Who hath delivered us from **the power of darkness,** *and hath translated us into the kingdom of his dear Son.* (Colossians 1:13)

principalities and powers
(political authorities or high positions)

Put them in mind to be subject to **principalities and powers,** *to obey magistrates, to be ready to every good work.* (Titus 3:1)

ravening wolves
(greedy and vicious people)

Beware of false prophets, which come to you in sheep's clothing, but inwardly they are <u>ravening wolves</u>. (Matthew 7:15)

reap the whirlwind
(to get into deeper trouble than you expect)

For they have sown the wind, and they shall <u>reap the whirlwind</u>: *it hath no stalk: the bud shall yield no meal: if so be it yield, the strangers shall swallow it up.* (Hosea 8:7)

reed shaken by the wind
(to have an opinion shaped by the times)

And as they departed, Jesus began to say unto the multitudes concerning John, What went ye out into the wilderness to see? <u>**A reed shaken with the wind**</u>? (Matthew 11:7)

riotous living
(a lifestyle of sin)

And not many days after the younger son gathered all together, and took his journey into a far country, and there wasted his substance with <u>riotous living</u>. (Luke 15:13)

sackcloth and ashes, put on
(to be repentant and humble)

And in every province, whithersoever the king's commandment and his decree came, there was great mourning among the Jews, and fasting, and weeping, and wailing; and many lay in <u>sackcloth and ashes</u>. (Esther 4:3)

set your face against

(to turn your mind against something or someone)

And I will **set my face against** *that man, and will cut him off from among his people; because he hath given of his seed unto Molech, to defile my sanctuary, and to profane my holy name.* (Leviticus 20:3)

shining light

(a prominent individual)

He was a burning and **a shining light***: and ye were willing for a season to rejoice in his light.* (John 5:35)

sin will find you out

(your bad deeds will be found out)

But if ye will not do so, behold, ye have sinned against the LORD*: and be sure your* **sin will find you out.** (Numbers 32:23)

sitting at the receipt of custom

(a money handler or cashier)

And as Jesus passed forth from thence, he saw a man, named Matthew, **sitting at the receipt of custom***: and he saith unto him, Follow me. And he arose, and followed him.* (Matthew 9:9)

slow to anger

(a good temperament; even keeled)

And refused to obey, neither were mindful of thy wonders that thou didst among them; but hardened their necks, and in their rebellion appointed a captain to return to their bondage: but thou art a God ready to pardon, gracious and merciful, **slow to anger,** *and of great kindness, and forsookest them not.* (Nehemiah 9:17)

smite them hip and thigh

(to savagely attack your enemies with anything)

And he **smote them hip and thigh** *with a great slaughter: and he went down and dwelt in the top of the rock Etam.* (Judges 15:8)

son of Belial

(a vile, wicked person)

Now the sons of Eli were **sons of Belial***; they knew not the* LORD. (1 Samuel 2:12)

sounding brass

(one who is all talk; a vain person)

Though I speak with the tongues of men and of angels, and have not charity, I am become as **sounding brass***, or a tinkling cymbal.* (1 Corinthians 13:1)

spoil the Egyptians

(ravage one's enemies)

But every woman shall borrow of her neighbor, and of her that sojour-neth in her house, jewels of silver, and jewels of gold, and raiment: and ye shall put them upon your sons, and upon your daughters; and ye shall **spoil the Egyptians.** (Exodus 3:22)

still small voice

(listening to your conscience)

And after the earthquake a fire; but the LORD *was not in the fire: and after the fire* **a still small voice***.* (1 Kings 19:12)

tell it not in Gath

(don't make something public knowledge)

<u>Tell it not in Gath,</u> *publish it not in the streets of Askelon; lest the daughters of the Philistines rejoice, lest the daughters of the uncircumcised triumph.* (2 Samuel 1:20)

thief in the night

(secretly; discreetly)

For yourselves know perfectly that the day of the Lord so cometh as <u>a thief in the night</u>*.* (1 Thessalonians 5:2)

tower of strength

(someone you can count on)

The name of the LORD is <u>a strong tower</u>*: the righteous runneth into it, and is safe.* (Proverbs 18:10)

valley of the shadow death

(to be near death)

Yea, though I walk through <u>the valley of the shadow of death</u>*, I will fear no evil: for thou art with me; thy rod and thy staff they comfort me.* (Psalm 23:4)

very present help
in time of trouble

(useful in time of need)

God is our refuge and strength, <u>a very present help in trouble</u>*.* (Psalm 46:1)

wars and rumors of wars

(actual war or news of it)

And ye shall hear of __wars and rumors of wars__*: see that ye be not troubled: for all these things must come to pass, but the end is not yet.* (Matthew 24:6)

way of the transgressor is hard

(the hard life of sin)

Good understanding giveth favor: but __the way of transgressors is hard__*.* (Proverbs 13:15)

weariness of the flesh

(something that tires you greatly)

And further, by these, my son, be admonished: of making many books there is no end; an much study is a __weariness of the flesh__*.* (Ecclesiastes 12:12)

well nigh

(almost)

But as for me, my feet were almost gone; my steps had __well nigh__ *slipped.* (Psalms 73:2)

whited sepulchre

(a hypocrite, especially religious)

Woe unto you, scribes and Pharisees, hypocrites! for ye are like unto __whited sepulchres__*, which indeed appear beautiful outward, but are within full of dead men's bones, and of all uncleanness.* (Matthew 23:27)

wings of the wind
(go at top speed rather quietly)

And he rode upon a cherub, and did fly: yea, he did fly upon the <u>wings of the wind</u>. (Psalm 18:10)

woman's glory
(long hair of a woman)

But if <u>a woman</u> *have long hair, it is a* <u>glory</u> *to her: for her hair is given her for a covering.* (1 Corinthians 11:15)

word in season
(saying the right thing at the right time)

A man hath joy by the answer of his mouth: and <u>a word</u> *spoken* <u>in</u> *due* <u>season</u>, *how good is it!* (Proverbs 15:23)

Appendix B
Popular Expressions
Alluded to in the Bible

all decked out
(dressed up fancily)

And I will visit upon her the days of Baalim, wherein she burned incense to them, and **she decked herself** *with her earrings and her jewels, and she went after her lovers, and forgat me, saith the LORD.* (Hosea 2:13)

all hope is lost
(an irreversible situation)

Now when she saw that she had waited, and her **hope was lost,** *then she took another of her whelps, and made him a young lion.* (Ezekiel 19:5)

all over but the shouting
(just about finished)

For the Lord himself shall **descend from heaven with a shout,** *with the voice of the archangel and with the trump of God: and the dead in Christ shall rise first.* (1 Thessalonians 4:16)

as long as there is life, there is hope
(always believe)

For to him that is joined to all **the living there is hope:** *for a living dog is better than a dead lion.* (Ecclesiastes 9:4)

blessing in disguise

(something thought to be bad turning out otherwise)

And he said, Thy brother <u>came with subtilty</u>, *and hath* <u>taken away thy blessing</u>. (Genesis 27:35)

blind faith

(believing without seeing)

Now <u>faith is</u> *the substance of things hoped for,* <u>the</u> *evidence of things not seen.* (Hebrews 11:1)

born to be wild

(natural inclinations for rebellion)

Yet man is <u>born</u> *un<u>to trouble</u>, as the sparks fly upward.* (Job 5:7)

bosom buddy

(close, dear friend)

Now there was leaning on Jesus' <u>bosom one of his disciples</u>, *whom Jesus loved.* (John 13:23)

bring down to earth

(make someone face reality)

The pride of thine heart hath deceived thee, thou that dwelleth in the clefts of the rock, whose habitation is high; that saith in his heart, Who shall <u>bring me down to the ground?</u> (Obadiah 3)

burn the midnight oil

(work late into the night)

*And at **midnight** there was a cry made, Behold, the bridegroom cometh; go ye out to meet him. Then all the virgins arose, and trimmed their lamps. And the foolish said unto the wise, Give us of your **oil**; for our lamps are gone out.* (Matthew 25:6–8)

can't call your soul your own

(to have you or your things controlled by others)

*What? know ye not that your body is the temple of the Holy Ghost which is in you, which ye have of God, and **ye are not your own**?* (1 Corinthians 6:19)

can't keep a good man down

(determined to not give up)

*The steps of **a good man** are ordered by the Lord, and he delighteth in his ways. Though he fall, he **shall not be utterly cast down**: for the LORD upholdeth him with his hand.* (Psalm 37:24–5)

can't see for the tears

(crying extensively)

Mine eyes do fail with tears, *my bowels are troubled, my liver is poured upon the earth, for the destruction of the daughter of my people; because the children and the sucklings swoon in the streets of the city.* (Lamentations 2:11)

captain of your soul

(you determine your own fate)

*For it became him, for whom are all things, and by whom are all things, in bringing many sons unto glory, to make **the captain of their salvation** perfect through sufferings.* (Hebrews 2:10)

charity begins at home

(take care of your family first)

But if any widow have children or nephews, let them learn first to shew piety **at home, and to requite their parents***: for that is good and acceptable before God.* (1 Timothy 5:4)

cover with a fig leaf

(to be chaste; to conceal the flesh)

And the eyes of them both were opened, and they knew that they were naked; and **they sewed fig leaves** *together,* **and made themselves aprons**. (Genesis 3:7)

cross my heart and hope to die

(kill me if I'm wrong)

And when all the people came to cause David to eat meat while it was yet day, David sware, saying, **So do God to me, and more also***, if I taste bread, or ought else, till the sun be down.* (2 Samuel 3:35)

dead end

(no improvement possible)

What fruit had ye then in those things whereof ye are now ashamed? for **the end of those things is death**. (Romans 6:21)

dead men tell no tales

(the dead can't reveal matters)

For the living know that they shall die: but **the dead know not any thing***, neither have they any more a reward; for the memory of them is forgotten.* (Ecclesiastes 9:5)

devil made me do it
(blaming others for your problems)

And the Lord *God said unto the woman, What is this that thou hast done? And the woman said,* **The serpent beguiled me, and I did eat.** (Genesis 3:13)

dig your own grave
(cause your own downfall or death)

He that diggeth a pit shall fall into it; *and whoso breaketh an hedge, a serpent shall bite him.* (Ecclesiastes 10:8)

do the little things
(giving attention to small matters)

He that is **faithful in that which is least** *is faithful also in much: and he that is unjust in the least is unjust also in much.* (Luke 16:10)

doubting Thomas
(someone who is always skeptical)

But Thomas, one of the twelve, called Didymus, was not with them when Jesus came. The other disciples therefore said unto him, We have seen the Lord. But he said unto them, **Except I shall see** *in his hands the print of the nails, and put my finger into the print of the nails, and thrust my hand into his side,* **I will not believe.** (John 20:24–5)

down in the mouth
(a sad countenance)

And the Lord said unto Cain, Why art thou wroth? And why is thy **countenance fallen**? (Genesis 4:6)

do your own thing

(follow your own dictates)

In those days there was no king in Israel, but **every man did that which was right in his own eyes**. (Judges 17:6)

drive you to your knees

(make someone suffer)

Terrors shall make him afraid on every side, and shall **drive him to his feet**. (Job 18:11)

eyes are the windows of the soul

(the eyes reveal things)

The light of the body is the eye: *if therefore thine eye be single, thy whole body shall be full of light.* (Matthew 6:22)

eyes of faith

(spiritual faith)

(For we **walk by faith, not by sight***)* (2 Corinthians 5:7)

eyes on the prize

(focused on a goal)

I press **toward the mark for the prize** *of the high calling of God in Christ Jesus.* (Philippians 3:14)

faith that moves mountains

(strong faith)

And Jesus said unto them, Because of your unbelief: for verily I say unto you, **If ye have faith** *as a grain of mustard seed,* **ye shall say unto**

this mountain, Remove hence to yonder place; *and it shall remove;
and nothing shall be impossible unto you.* (Matthew 17:20)

fate worse than death
(damnation of hell)

*And fear not them which kill the body, but are not able to kill the soul:
but rather* **fear him which is able to destroy both soul and body in
hell.** *(Matthew 10:28)*

father knows best
(the parent knows children's needs)

Be not ye therefore like unto them: for **your Father knoweth** *what
things ye have need of, before ye ask him.* (Matthew 6:8)

forbidden fruit
(that which is forbidden yet tempting)

But of **the fruit of the tree** *which is in the midst of the garden, God
hath said,* **Ye shall not eat of it,** *neither shall ye touch it, lest ye die.*
(Genesis 3:3)

full of yourself
(conceited)

The backslider in heart **shall be filled with his own ways:** *and a good
man shall be satisfied from himself.* (Proverbs 14:14)

go through the motions
(mechanical, unemotional activity)

For **when we were in the flesh, the motions of sins,** *which were by* *the law, did work in our members to bring forth fruit unto death.* (Romans 7:5)

go to your reward

(get what you deserve)

Therefore when thou doest thine alms, do not sound a trumpet before thee, as the hypocrites do in the synagogues and in the streets, that they may have glory of men. Verily I say unto you, They **have their reward**. (Matthew 6:2)

good Samaritan

(someone who helps others in need)

But **a certain Samaritan**, *as he journeyed, came where he was: and when he saw him, he* **had compassion on him**. (Luke 10:33)

have nothing on someone

(to have no accusations on another)

Hereafter I will not talk much with you: for the prince of this world cometh, and **hath nothing in me**. (John 14:30)

haven't got a prayer

(hopeless)

Thou hast covered thyself with a cloud, that **our prayer should not pass through**. (Lamentations 3:44)

hearing footsteps

(listening for those behind you)

But Elisha sat in his house, and the elders sat with him; and the king sent a man from before him: but ere the messenger came to him, he said to the elders, See ye how this son of a murderer hath sent to take away mine head? look, when the messenger cometh, shut the door, and hold him fast at the door: is not **the sound of his master's feet behind him?** (2 Kings 6:32)

hear no evil, see no evil, speak no evil

(not involved)

For he that will love life, and see good days, let him **refrain his tongue from evil, and his lips that they speak no guile.** (1 Peter 3:10)

heaven's gate

(entrance to heaven)

And he was afraid, and said, How dreadful is this place! this is none other but the house of God, and this is **the gate of heaven.** (Genesis 28:17)

he's asking for it

(looking for trouble)

A fool's lips enter into contention, and **his mouth calleth for strokes.** (Proverbs 18:6)

he who laughs last laughs best

(final revenge)

He *that sitteth in the heavens* **shall laugh:** *the Lord shall have them in derision.* (Psalm 2:4)

history repeats itself

(cyclical repetition of events)

<u>**The thing that hath been, it is that which shall be;**</u> *and that which is done is that which shall be done: and there is no new thing under the sun.* (Ecclesiastes 1:9)

keep body and soul together

(keep yourself fit)

And the very God of peace sanctify you wholly; and I pray God your whole spirit and <u>**soul and body be preserved blameless**</u> *unto the coming of our Lord Jesus Christ.* (1 Thessalonians 5:23)

king of the mountain

(ruler or leader)

And many people shall go up and say, Come ye, and let us go up to <u>**the mountain of the LORD,**</u> *to the house of the God of Jacob; and he will teach us of his ways, and we will walk in his paths: for out of Zion shall go forth the law, and the word of the LORD from Jerusalem.* (Psalm 48:2)

kiss of death

(the *coup de grace*)

Now <u>**he that betrayed him**</u> *gave them a sign, saying, Whomsoever* <u>**I shall kiss,**</u> *that same is he: hold him fast.* (Matthew 26:48)

know of what you speak

(learned)

Verily, verily, I say unto thee, <u>**We speak that we do know,**</u> *and testify that we have seen; and ye receive not our witness.* (John 3:11)

life's tough, and then you die
(life is hard with no reward)

This is an evil among all things that are done under the sun, that there is one event unto all: yea, also the heart of the sons of men is full of evil, and and <u>madness is in their heart while they live, and after that they go to the dead.</u> (Ecclesiastes 9:3)

like produces like
(expected results)

And God said, let the earth bring forth grass, the herb yielding seed, and <u>the fruit tree yielding fruit after his kind,</u> *whose seed is in itself, upon the earth: and it was so.* (Genesis 1:11)

long arm of the law
(authority figure)

Yet they are thy people and thine inheritance, which thou broughtest out by thy mighty power and <u>by thy stretched out arm.</u> (Deuteronomy 9:29)

look out for yourself
(selfish interests only)

Yea, they are greedy dogs which can never have enough, and they are shepherds that cannot understand: <u>they all look to their own way,</u> *every one for his gain, from his quarter.* (Isaiah 56:11)

man of few words
(a reserved individual)

Be not rash with thy mouth, and let not thine heart be hasty to utter any thing before God: for God is in heaven, and thou upon earth: there-fore <u>let thy words be few.</u> (Ecclesiastes 5:2)

marked man
(a person targeted for something)

And the LORD *said unto him, Therefore whosoever slayeth Cain, vengeance shall be taken on him sevenfold,* **And the** LORD **set a mark upon Cain,** *lest any finding him should kill him.* (Genesis 4:15)

marriage made in heaven
(a perfect marriage)

And he saith unto me, Write, Blessed are they which are called unto **the marriage supper of the Lamb.** *And he saith unto me, These are the true sayings of God.* (Revelation 19:9)

mountaintop experience
(spiritual encounter)

And after six days Jesus taketh Peter, James, and John his brother, and **bringeth them up into an high mountain apart. And was transfig-ured before them**: *and his face did shine as the sun, and his raiment was white as the light.* (Matthew 17:1–2)

move heaven and earth
(produce almost impossible results)

And **the heaven departed** *as a scroll when it is rolled together;* **and every mountain and island were moved** *out of their places.* (Revelation 6:14)

music soothes the savage beast
(goodness tempers evil)

Let our lord now command thy servants, which are before thee, to seek out a man, who is a cunning player on an harp: and it shall come to pass, **when the evil spirit from God is upon thee, that he shall play with his hand, and thou shalt be well.** (1 Samuel 16:16)

no big deal
(not overly important)

Therefore **it is no great thing** *if his ministers also be transformed as the ministers of righteousness; whose end shall be according to their works.* (2 Corinthians 11:15)

none so blind as those who won't see
(purposeful ignorance)

And Jesus said, For judgment I am come into this world, that they which see not might see; **and that they which see might be made blind.** (John 9:39)

no pain, no gain
(no sacrifice, no achieving)

If we suffer, we shall also reign *with him: if we deny him, he also will deny us.* (2 Timothy 2:12)

play with fire
(involve yourself with danger)

Can a man **take fire in his bosom,** *and his clothes not be burned?* (Proverbs 6:27)

pocket has holes in it
(spending and not saving)

Ye have sown much, and bring in little; ye eat, but ye have not enough; ye drink, but ye are not filled with drink; ye clothe you, but there in none warm; and he that earneth wages earneth wages to **put it into a bag with holes.** (Haggai 1:6)

put out to pasture

(put out of commission)

And they shall drive thee from men, and **thy dwelling shall be with the beasts of the field:** *they shall make thee to eat grass as oxen, and seven times shall pass over thee, until thou know that the most High ruleth in the kingdom of men, and giveth it to whomsoever he will.* (Daniel 4:32)

put someone's lights out

(to stop another completely)

The light of the righteous rejoiceth: but **the lamp of the wicked shall be put out.** (Proverbs 13:9)

rest in peace

(die or be left alone)

Therefore did my heart rejoice, and my tongue was glad; moreover also **my flesh shall rest in hope.** (Acts 2:26)

sadder but wiser

(knowledge through sadness)

For in much wisdom is much grief: and **he that increaseth knowledge increaseth sorrow.** (Ecclesiastes 1:18)

scrape the bottom of the barrel

(barely make ends meet)

And she said, As the LORD *thy God liveth, I have not a cake,* **but an handful of meal in a barrel,** *and a little oil in a cruse: and, behold, I am gathering two sticks, that I may go in and dress it for me and my son, that we may eat it, and die.* (1 Kings 17:2)

second coming
(Jesus' return; resurrection)

And if I go and prepare a place for you, **I will come again,** *and receive you unto myself; that where I am, there ye may be also.* (John 14:3)

sick at the sight of someone
(to despise another)

Behold, the hope of him is in vain: shall not one be **cast down even at the sight of him?** (Job 41:9)

stink in your nostrils
(abhor something)

I have sent among you the pestilence after the manner of Egypt: your young men have I slain with the sword, and have taken away your horses; and I **have made the stink of your camps to come up unto your nostrils:** *yet have ye not returned unto me, saith the* LORD. (Amos 4:10)

take the bitter with the sweet
(take the good with the bad)

And I went unto the angel, and said unto him, Give me the little book. And he said unto me, Take it, and eat it up; and **it shall make thy belly bitter, but it shall be in thy mouth sweet as honey.** (Revelation 10:9)

there is a time and place for every-thing
(there is a set time for all endeavors)

To **every thing there is a season,** *and a time to every purpose under the heaven.* (Ecclesiastes 3:1)

too much of a good thing is bad
(excess is harmful)

<u>It is not good to eat much honey</u>: so *for men* to search their own glory *is not* glory. (Proverbs 25:27)

turn a deaf ear
(not listen)

<u>He that turneth away his ear from hearing</u> law, even his prayer *shall be* abomination. (Proverbs 28:9)

water under the bridge
(forgotten grief)

Because thou shalt forget thy misery, and <u>remember it as waters that pass away.</u> (Job 11:16)

what's it to you?
(asking the relevance of a matter)

Saying, I have sinned in that I have betrayed the innocent blood. And they said, <u>What is that to us?</u> *See thou to that.* (Matthew 27:4)

when the spirit moves you
(when you feel like it)

And <u>the spirit of the LORD began to move him</u> *at times in the camp of Dan between Zorah and Eshtaol.* (Judges 13:25)

which ever way the wind blows
(swayed easily)

<u>The wind bloweth where it listeth,</u> *and thou hearest the sound*

thereof, but canst not tell whence it cometh, and whither it goeth: so is every one that is born of the Spirit. (John 3:8)

wish you'd never been born
(despise your life)

The Son of man indeed goeth, as it is written of him: but woe to that man by whom the Son of man is betrayed! **good were it for that man if he had never been born**. (Mark 14:21)

woman's place is in the home
(women should work in the home)

I will therefore, that **the younger women marry, bear children, guide the house**, *give none occasion to the adversary to speak reproachfully.* (1 Timothy 5:14)

wouldn't trust him to watch my dog
(not trust someone at all)

But now they that are younger than I have me in derision, whose fathers **I would have disdained to have set with the dogs of my flock**. (Job 30:1)

Appendix C
Popular Biblical Expressions In Movie and TV Titles

Amy Prentiss-Baptism of Fire (1974) Jessica Walter, William Shatner

And Nothing But the Truth (1982) Glenda Jackson, Jon Finch

Blind Faith (1988) Shelley Hack, Jack Langedyk

Body and Soul (1981) Muhammad Ali, Leon Kennedy, Peter Lawford

Born Again (1978) Dean Jones, Anne Francis

Brother's Keeper (1992) Joe Berlinger, Bruce Sinofsky

Brotherly Love (1969) Peter O'Toole, Susannah York

Burnt Offerings (1976) Bette Davis, Burgess Meredith

Call It a Day (1937) Olivia de Havilland, Ian Hunter

Cry in the Wilderness (1974) George Kennedy, Paul Sorenson

Dead and Buried (1981) James Farentino, Jack Albertson

Dead End (1937) Joel McCrea, Humphrey Bogart

Dead Men Tell No Tales (1971) Christopher George, Judy Carne

Dead to the World (1961) Reedy Talton, Jana Pearce

Death Sentence (1974) Cloris Leachman, Laurence Luckinbill

Dirty Money (1972) Alain Delon, Catherine Deneuve, Richard Crenna

Don't Take It to Heart (1945) Richard Greene, Patricia Medina

Don't Turn the Other Cheek (1973) Franco Nero, Lynn Redgrave

Doubting Thomas (1935) Will Rogers, Billie Burke

Biblical Expressions in Movie and TV Titles

End of the World (1977) Christopher Lee, Sire Lyon, Lew Ayers

Ends of the Earth (1981) Chuck Norris, Christopher Lee

Every Man for Himself (1980) Jacques Dutronc

Evil (Under the Sun) (1982) Peter Ustinov, Roddy McDowell

Evil Eye, The (1964) John Saxon, Leticia Roman

Eye for an Eye, An (1996) Sally Field

Eye of the Needle (1981) Donald Sutherland, Kate Nelligan

Face to Face (1976) Liv Ullman, Erland Josephson

Fallen Angel (1981) Richard Massur, Dana Hill

Falling from Grace (1992) John Mellencamp, Mariel Hemingway

Fire Down Below (1957) Rita Hayworth, Robert Mitchum

First Love (1977) William Kaat, Susan Dey, John Heard

Flesh and Blood (1985) Jennifer Leigh, Tom Burlinson

Forbidden Fruit (1958) Fernandel, Francoise Arnoul

Good Fight, The (1992) Christine Lahti, Terry O'Quinn

Gospel According to Vic, The (1986) Tom Conti, Helen Mirren

Green Pastures, The (1936) Marc Connelly, Rex Ingram

Hand in Hand (1960) Loretta Parey, Philip Needs

He Laughed Last (1956) Frankie Lane, Lucy Marlow

Hear No Evil (1993) Marlee Matlin, Martin Sheen

Heart and Souls (1993) Robert Downey Jr., Charles Grodin

Heart of the Matter, The (1953) Trevor Howard

Hearts and Minds (1934) Peter Davis, Dir.

Heaven on Earth (1986) R. H. Thompson, Sian Leisa Davies

High and the Mighty, The (1954) John Wayne, Claire Trevor, Robert Stack

Biblical Expressions in Movie and TV Titles

High Noon (1952) Gary Cooper, Grace Kelly

High Time (1960) Bing Crosby, Fabian, Tuesday Weld

Holy Terror (1977) Brooke Shields, Tom Signorelli

House Divided, A (1932) Walter Huston, Kent Douglas

In God We Trust (1980) Marty Feldman, Peter Boyle, Richard Pryor

In the Cool of the Day (1963) Peter Finch, Jane Fonda, Angela Lansbury

In the Spirit (1990) Marlo Thomas, Peter Falk

Joy in the Morning (1965) Richard Chamberlain, Yvette Mimieux

Judgment Day (1988) Kenneth McLeod, David Anthony Smith

Kiss of Death (1947) Victor Mature, Brian Dunleavy, Richard Widmark

Last Laugh, The (1924) Emil Jannings

Law of the Land (1976) Jim Davis, Barbara Parkins, Don Johnson

Left Hand of God, The (1955) Humphrey Bogart, Gene Tiernes, Lee J. Cobb

Light of Day (1987) Michael J. Fox, Joan Jett, Gena Rowlands

Like Father, Like Son (1987) Dudley Moore, Kirk Cameron

Lost and Found (1979) George Segal, Glenda Jackson, John Candy

Made in Heaven (1987) Timothy Hutton, Kelly McGillis

Man of the House (1995) Chevy Chase, Farrah Fawcett

Man of the World (1931) Carole Lombard, William Powell

Man, Woman, and Child (1983) Martin Sheen, Craig T. Nelson

Merrily We Go to Hell (1932) Fredric March, Sylvia Sidney, Cary Grant

My Brother's Keeper (1948) Jack Warner, George C. Scott

Next of Kin (1989) Patrick Swayze, Liam Neeson, Adam Baldwin, Helen Hunt

Nothing But the Truth (1941) Bob Hope, Paulette Goddard

Out of Season (1975) Vanessa Redgrave, Cliff Robinson

Biblical Expressions in Movie and TV Titles

Out of Sight, Out of Mind (1990) Susan Blakely, Wings Hauser

Out of the Body (1988) Mark Hembrow, Tessa Humphries

Passed Away (1992) Bob Hoskins, Jack Warden

Playing with Fire (1985) Gary Coleman, Cicely Tyson

Promised Land (1988) Kiefer Sutherland, Meg Ryan

Quick and the Dead, The (1995) Sharon Stone, Gene Hackman

Rest in Pieces (1987) Scott Thompson, Lorin Jean

Rise and Fall of Legs Diamond, The (1960) Ray Danton, Karen Steele, Warren Oates

Rise and Shine (1941) Walter Brennan, Milton Berle

Sacred Ground (1983) Tim McIntire, Jack Elam

Salt of the Earth (1954) Will Greer, Mervin Williams

Samaritan: The Mitch Snyder Story (1972) Barry Norman, Anne Karina

Saving Grace (1986) Tom Conti, Fernando Rey

Sign o' the Times (1987) Prince, Sheila E., Sheena Easton

Sins of the Fathers (1986) Burt Lancaster, Julie Christie

Smooth Talk (1985) Treat Williams, Laura Dern

Spare the Rod (1961) Max Bygraves, Donald Pleaseance

Spirit is Willing, The (1967) Sid Caesar, Vera Miles

Star Trek **(Episode 68): *Wink of an Eye*** (1969) William Shatner, Leonard Nimoy

They Ran for Their Lives (1969) John Payne, Jim Davis

Through a Glass Darkly (1961) Max Von Sydow, Harriet Anderson

Turning to Stone (1985) Nicky Guadagni, Shirley Douglas

Way of All Flesh, The (1940) Akim Tamiroff, Gladys George

You Can't Take It with You (1984) Jason Robards Jr., George Rose

Appendix D
Popular Biblical Expressions in Song Titles

"**A Cross to Bear**" by Iain Matthews

"**A Little Bird Told Me**" by Evelyn Knight

"**Apple of My Eye**" by Badfinger

"**As God is My Witness**" by Toadstool

"**Baptism by Fire**" by Ann DeJarnett

"**Blink of an Eye**" by Michael McDonald

"**Breach of Promise**" by Pell Mell

"**Bread and Wine**" by Peter Gabriel

"**Break of Dawn**" by Salt-N-Pepa

"**Breaking the Law**" by Judas Priest

"**Brother's Keeper**" by 12 Gauge

"**Brotherly Love**" by Moe Bandy

"**By and By When I Need You**" by New Riders of the Purple Sage

"**By the Book**" by Michael Penn

"**By the Sweat of Your Brow**" by The Heptones

"**Cast the First Stone**" by Angel

"**Crystal Clear**" by The Mighty Lemon Drops

"**Dead and Gone**" by Molly Hatchet

"**Dead End**" by Dead Kennedys

"**Dearly Beloved**" by Fred Astaire

"**Den of Thieves**" by Lizzy Borden

"**Die by the Sword**" by Slayer

"**Drop in the Bucket**" by David Lee Roth

"**Eat My Words**" by Taste

"**End of the World**" by Pet Shop Boys

"**Everybody Plays the Fool**" by The Main Ingredient

"**Evil Eye**" by Gino Vanelli

"**Eye for an Eye**" by Corrosion of Conformity

"**Eye to Eye**" by Joan Jett

"**Eyesight to the Blind**" by B. B. King

"**Faith Can Move Mountains**" by Nat King Cole

"**Fall From Grace**" by Siouxsie and the Banshees

"**Fallen Angel**" by Blue Oyster Cult

"**Falling by the Wayside**" by Ramblers

"**Fear and Loathing at 4th and Butternut**" by John Fahey

"**Fight the Good Fight**" by Triumph

"**Fire and Brimstone**" by Joe Walsh

"**First Love**" by Poco

"**Flesh and Blood**" by Johnny Cash

"**Fly in the Ointment**" by The Faces

"**For God's Sake**" by Cut to the Chase

"**For the Love of Money**" by the O'Jays

"**Forty Days and Forty Nights**" by Muddy Waters

"**Fuel to the Flame**" by Skeeter Davis

"**Give up the Ghost**" by The Le Roi Brothers

"**Go to Hell**" by Alice Cooper

"**God Save the Queen**" by Sex Pistols

"**Good for Nothing**" by Marlene Dietrich

"**Hard Headed Woman**" by Cat Stevens

"**Heart and Soul**" by Mel Torme

Biblical Expressions in Song Titles

"Heart of Stone" by The Rolling Stones

"Heart's Desire" by The Manhattan Transfer

"Hearts and Minds" by Ebb Nitzer

"Heaven on Earth" by Asia

"Heavy Heart" by Heart

"Here and There" by Sandbox

"Here Today and Gone Tomorrow" by Earth, Wind & Fire

"High Noon" by Tex Ritter

"High Time" by Styx

"Hold Your Tongue Dear Sally" by Andy M. Stewart

"Hole in My Pocket" by Rickey Van Shelton

"Holier Than Thou" by Metallica

"Holy Water" by Soundgarden

"House Divided" by Dry Branch Fire Squad

"Hung the Moon" by Better than Ezra

"In God We Trust" by Those X-Cleavers

"Iron Hand" by Dire Straits

"Ivory Tower" by Cathy Carr

"Keep the Faith" by Michael Jackson

"Kingdom Come" by David Bowie

"Know It All" by Wes Montgomery

"Labor of Love" by Robert Cray

"Land of Milk and Honey" by Dizzy Gillespie

"Land of the Giants" by Craig Chaquico

"Land of the Living" by Don Henley

"Laughing on Judgment Day" by Thunder

"Law of the Land" by The Temptations

"Like Father Like Son" by Rick Springfield

"Little by Little" by Alice Cooper

"Lord, Have Mercy on My Soul" by Black Oak Arkansas

"Lost and Found" by The Kinks

"Love Thy Neighbor" by Bing Crosby

"Make a Scene" by Chris Bell

"Man of the House" by Loretta Lynn

"Man of the World" by Fleetwood Mac

"Many a Time" by Common Man Singers

"Meet Your Maker" by Bitter End

"Mind Your Own Business" by Hank Williams, Jr.

"My Cup Runneth Over" by George Jones

"My Heart is an Open Book" by Carl Dobkins, Jr.

"My Heart's Desire" by The Earls

"Name in Vain" by Motorhead

"Night is Still Young" by Billy Joel

"Nothin' New Under the Sun" by Inner Circle

"One Way or Another" by Blondie

"Out of Season" by R.E.O. Speedwagon

"Out of Sight, Out of Mind" by Elvis Presley

"Out of the Body" by Pestilence

"Parting of Our Ways" by the Carpenters

"Passed Away" by Desultory

"Passing the Time" by Cream

"Patience Like Job" by Sunnyland Slim Blues Band

"Patience of a Saint" by Electronic Band

"Peace and Quiet Time" by Mike Fahn

"Peace of Mind" by Teresa Brewer

"Peace on Earth" by David Bowie and Bing Crosby

Biblical Expressions in Song Titles

"**Pearly Gates**" by Blind Willie McTell

"**Putty (in Your Hands)**" by The Shirelles

"**Reap the Whirlwind**" by Don Pullen

"**Reap What You Sow**" by The Pastels

"**Rest for the Weary**" by Marc Cohn

"**Rest in Peace**" by Mott the Hoople

"**Rise and Shine**" by Pink Floyd

"**Root of All Evil**" by Sacred Denial

"**Run For Your Life**" by The Beatles

"**Sackcloth and Ashes**" by The Mr. T. Experience

"**Safe and Sound**" by Carly Simon

"**Salt of the Earth**" by Joan Baez

"**Saving Grace**" by Bob Dylan

"**Scum of the Earth**" by The Kinks

"**See the Light**" by Jeff Healey Band

"**Seeing is Believing**" by Mike and the Mechanics

"**Skin O' My Teeth**" by Megadeth

"**Stone's Throw from Hurtin'**" by Elton John

"**Straight and Narrow**" by Paul Overstreet

"**Stranger in a Strange Land**" by U2

"**Streets of Gold**" by The Fabulous Thunderbirds

"**Stumbling Block Blues**" by Champion Jack DuPree

"**Such and Such**" by 7 Seconds

"**Sweatin' Bullets**" by Brand Nubian

"**Take It Easy**" by the Eagles

"**Tell It Like It Is**" by Bad Company

"**Tender Mercies**" by Scott Kempner

"**The Eleventh Hour**" by Mars Lasar

Biblical Expressions in Song Titles

"The End is Near" by Leaders of the New School

"The Extra Mile" by Tom Russell

"The Good Lord" by The Abyssinians

"The Gospel According to Darkness" by Jane Siberry

"The Heart of the Matter" by Kenny Rogers

"The Heat of the Battle" by Roy Buchanan

"The High and the Mighty" by Leroy Holmes

"The Powers That Be" by Roger Waters

"The Promised Land" by Chuck Berry

"The Ten Commandments of Love" by Little Anthony and the Imperials

"There is No Greater Love" by Billie Holiday

"Thorn in My Side" by the Eurythmics

"Through a Glass Dimly" by Jeff Beal

"To the Ends of the Earth" by Nat King Cole

"Tossin' and Turnin'" by Bobby Lewis

"Turned to Stone" by Electric Light Orchestra

"Two Heads Are Better Than One" by Power Tool

"Under My Wings" by James Taylor

"Voice in the Wilderness" by Unshakable Race

"Wages of Sin" by Pegboy

"Walk Hand in Hand" by Tony Martin

"Woe is Me" by The Cadillacs

"Writing on the Wall" by Ted Nugent

"Written in Stone" by Daryl Hall

"You Can't Take It With You" by Ray Price

"You're Breakin' My Heart" by Vic Damone

"Your Days Are Numbered" by Big Chief

Bibliography

Ammer, Christine. *Have a Nice Day—No Problem!* New York: Penguin Books USA Inc., 1992.

Castell, Ron, editor. *Blockbuster Video Guide to Movies and Videos 1996.* New York: Dell Publishing, 1995.

Claiborne, Robert. *Loose Cannons and Red Herrings: A Book of Lost Metaphors.* New York: W.W. Norton Company, 1988.

Craig, Doris. *Catch Phrases, Clichés, and Idioms.* Jefferson, North Carolina: McFarland and Company, Inc., 1990.

Dictionary of Phrase and Fable. New Lanark, Scotland: Brock-hampton Press, 1995.

Doege, Danny C. *Why We Say, What We Say!* No Publisher, 1994.

Ehrlich, Eugene, and David H. Scott. *Mene, Mene, Tekel.* New York: HarperCollins Publishers, 1990.

Evans, Ivor H., editor. *Brewer's Dictionary of Phrase and Fable.* 14 ed. New York: Harper and Row Publishers, 1989.

Kirkpatrick, E. M. and C.M. Schwarz editors. *The Wordsworth Dictionary of Idioms.* Ware, Hertfordshire: Wordsworth Editions Ltd., 1993.

Lass, Abraham H., David Kiremedjran, and Ruth M. Goldstein. *The Dictionary of Classical, Biblical and Literary Allusions.* New York: Ballantine Books, 1987.

Macrone, Michael. *Brush Up Your Bible!* New York: HarperCollins Publishers, 1993.

Bibliography

Maltin, Leonard, editor. *TV Movies and Video Guide.* 1989 Edition. New York: NAL Penguin Inc., 1988.

Manser, Martin H. editor. *I Never Knew That Was in the Bible.* Nashville: Thomas Nelson Publishers, 1999.

McNeil, Alex. *Total Television.* 3rd rev. ed. New York: Viking Penguin, 1991.

Partridge, Eric. *A Dictionary of Clichés with an Introductory Essay.* 5th ed. New York: Routledge and Kegan Ltd., 1978.

Rogers, James. *The Dictionary of Clichés.* New York: Ballantine Books, 1985.

Rosenthal, Peggy and George Dardess. *Every Cliché in the Book.* New York: William Morrow and Company, Inc., 1987

Simpson, J.A., ed. *The Concise Oxford Dictionary of Proverbs.* New York: Oxford University Press, 1982.

Smyth, Alice Mary et al. *The Oxford Dictionary of Quotations.* 2nd ed. New York: Oxford University Press, 1955.

Terrace, Vincent. *The Complete Encyclopedia of Television Programs 1947–1979.* 2d ed. rev. 2 vols. New York: A. S. Barnes and Company, Inc., 1979.

Wright, Larry. *Happy as a Clam and 9,999 Other Similes.* New York: Prentice Hall General Reference, 1994.